BLACK COP

by
INA R. FRIEDMAN

P.O. Box 1259
BROOKLINE, MA
02146 - 0010
Tel. 617-277-2323
Fax. 617-277-4592

PHOTO CREDITS: *Ebony* magazine, P. 103; FBI, p.112;
Metropolitan Police Dept., Washington, D.C., pp.2, 106,
114, 130, 140, 145, 150, 152;UPI, p.119; *Washington
Evening Star*, p.117; *The Washington Post*, pp.127, 128, 143.
All other photos courtesy of the O'Bryant family.

Front Cover/ Assistant Chief Tilmon O'Bryant.
Book Design by Dorothy Alden Smith

Published by Lodgepole Press, Brookline, Massachusetts
P.O. Box 1259 Brookline, MA. 02146
http://www.tiac.net/users/starobin/

PRINTED IN THE UNITED STATES OF AMERICA

Library of Congress Cataloging in Publication Data

Friedman, Ina R.
Black cop.
Summary: A biography of Tilmon B. O'Bryant who
battled racial barriers to rise to the position of Assistant
Chief of Police in Washington, D.C.
  1. O'Bryant, Tilmon B. 2. African-American policemen-
Biography-Juvenile literature. [O'Bryant, Tilmon B.
3. District of Columbia police-civil rights movement]
4. Civil rights, District of Columbia, 1930-1970.

CIP #: 96 - 79044
ISBN: 1-886721-01-7

A word from the Mayor of Washington, D.C.

Every city has its heroes. Tilmon B. O'Bryant is one of ours. He is one of those officers who is making the Metropolitan Police Department of the Nation's Capital the finest. He is dedicated to ensuring justice through law to the total community.

BLACK COP tells of his determination to overcome the many obstacles which sought to deter him. It is an exciting story, reflecting the challenges of urban life in the Twentieth Century.

It should inspire many young people to seek careers in law enforcement, as well as to serve in others areas of government.

October 18, 1973

My special thanks to Margot Stern Strom, Director, Facing History & Ourselves, for encouraging me to issue this new edition of *Black Cop*. I am also indebted to Jo Ann Butler Henry, Thelma Gruenbaum, Tracey O'Brien, Natalie Rothstein, Rob Winston, Sam D. Starobin and Robert Smyth for their assistance.

OTHER BOOKS BY INA R. FRIEDMAN

Flying Against The Wind: The Story of a Young Woman Who Defied the Nazis (Lodgepole Press). A stunning biography of a young German whose extraordinary courage and sense of justice led her to join the handful of non-Jewish Germans who resisted Hitler. $11.95 soft cover , ISBN: 1-886721-00-9. Glossary, Index, Bibliography.
"Informative inspirational, and exciting... would make an excellent companion piece to the study of Anne Frank's diary... should be in all libraries." Kliatt Review
"A powerful biography of a young girl's coming-of-age in Nazi Germany.... A role model for today's teenagers."Margot Stern Strom, Director, Facing History and Ourselves. NCSS Notable; Honorable Mention, Sugarman Award

The Other Victims: First Person Stories of Non-Jews Persecuted by the Nazis, ISBN: 0-395-74515-2. NCSS Notable; ALA Best Books for Young Adults; American Bookseller, Pick of The Lists. $5.95, soft cover, $14.95 hard cover.

Escape or Die: True Stories of Young People Who Defied the Nazis, ISBN: 0-938756-34-6, $10.95 "... demonstrates the remarkable resilience of the human spirit... a reminder that childhood is no defense against political policies engendered by hatred... Powerful and absorbing,... a notable addition to the literature of the Holocaust." Horn Book

Available through local bookstores or through Lodgepole Press, P.O. Box 1259, Brookline, MA 02146. For mail orders please add $2.50 for postage and handling for the first book, for each aditional book add $1.00 postage. Orders of five or more books sent postage free.

PREFACE

On April 4, 1968, the tragic news of Dr. Martin Luther King's assassination reverberated throughout the city of Washington, D.C. Smoke filled the streets as fires, set by angry and frustrated African-Americans, burned a few blocks from the White House. In Chevy Chase, Maryland, National Guardsmen patrolled the "border" between the city and the suburbs. I was devastated by these events, and I realized the necessity for tearing down the walls of fear and suspicion between races. The first place to start was with my own children and their friends.

After the riots, I went to my library in Bethesda, Maryland, to find books on black heroes for my children, who are white. I felt that history was biased in the absence of stories of African-American achievements. All I found were books on George Washington Carver, black athletes or musicians. While these were fine examples these individuals had special talents. I was seeking stories of ordinary people, men and women in the day to day jobs with which my children could identify such as policemen, teachers, government workers or nurses.

Then I thought of Tilmon B. O'Bryant, the first African-American to become assistant chief of police in the District of Columbia.

A frequent guest in my home, Tilmon always told my children stories of his detective work. They were fascinated, and they admired his perseverance despite the attempts of a racially biased police force to hold him back.

Tilmon's life, detailing his rise from welfare and the ghetto to assistant chief of police, reveals what it was like to grow up black and poor in Washington, D.C. It relates his struggle to achieve a place in the police department, not only for himself, but for future generations of all races. His story reflects the struggles in the civil rights movement, through one man's personal battle for justice, in the nation's capital from the 1950's to 1973.

When Tilmon was asked, "Why did you let a white woman write your biography?" He replied, "No black person ever asked me."

The first edition of this book appeared in 1974. At that time, African-Americans identified themselves as blacks or colored. To reflect the language of the times, I have left the text as originally printed.

AFRICAN-AMERICANS
AND THE NATION'S CAPITAL: 1791-1974

From Slavery to a Black Mayor

African-Americans participated in the development of the federal city of Washington, D.C. from its very beginning. From Benjamin Bannecker, a self-educated freed slave, who helped lay out the streets and boundaries of the new city of Washington to Walter E. Washington who became mayor in 1967, African-Americans have played a role in the growth of the nation's capital from an eighteenth century village of unpaved streets and open sewers to one of the world's most beautiful capitals. Some were among the freed persons who flocked to the city. Others were slaves hired out by their masters to contractors to construct the Capitol and the White House.

The former slaves pouring into the capital realized that only with education could they hope for better jobs and lives. In 1807, three former slaves established the first school for black children in the nation's capital. From a handful of such schools, the African-American community by the mid-1800's had produced ministers, teachers, a clerk to Smithsonian Institution and assistants to the Librarian of Congress.

When Congress abolished slavery in the District of Columbia in 1862, more African-Americans flocked to the city. A Freedman's Aid Society was established in 1862 to help the former slaves, and in 1863, the community rejoiced when President Lincoln issued the emancipation proclamation abolishing slavery.

The hopes of the freedmen and women for true equality rose at the end of the Civil War when Congress passed a series of amendments to the Constitution. The thirteenth amendment outlawed slavery. The fourteenth assured all Americans of "equal protection under the law". The fifteenth stated that all men "regardless of color" had the right to vote. In 1875 the Civil Rights Act legislated that all persons, regardless of color, were entitled to equal accommodations.

However, a political backlash soon set in. The Supreme Court declared that the Civil Rights Act of 1875 was unconstitutional and many states passed "Jim Crow" laws preventing African-Americans from voting or obtaining equal access to education or jobs. Washington remained a segregated city until well into the 1960's when Congress passed the Civil Rights Acts.

Though the struggle for equality was pushed back, two institutions of learning, Dunbar High School and Howard University, excelled in the education they offered their pupils. From among their faculty and their student body came such distinguished African-Americans as Dr. Ralph Bunche, a US Ambassador; Thurgood Marshall, a justice to the U.S. Supreme Court; Dr. Charles Drew, the developer of a system of preserving blood plasma for transfusions; Andrew Young, the civil rights leader, ambassador to the United Nations and the former mayor of Atlanta, Georgia, and many other distinguished men and women.

The unequal status of African Americans in Washington was reflected in the city's political structure. Since the 1870's, the city had been governed by three commissioners appointed by the President with the approval of the Senate. Though African-Americans made up a majority in the city, they had little role in its government.

In 1967, President Johnson decided to correct this inequity. He could not change the structure of the city's government because it was determined by Congress which was unwilling to modify the system. To by-pass Congress, President Johnson dismissed the three commissioners and appointed an African-American, Walter Washington, as the sole commissioner to be known as the mayor-commissioner. In 1972, Congress formalized this change by granting the people of Washington the right to elect their own leaders, a mayor and a city council. In the historic election of 1974, Walter Washington became the first African-American to be elected the head of the District of Columbia Government.

CONTENTS

GLOSSARY

Blitzkrieg-A lightning-like military attack.

CCC- Civilian Conservation Corps. A program set up to give work to unemployed young men.

Civil Rights Commission-A government agency set up to guarantee civil rights.

Civil Rights Drive-A movement to register voters and eliminate segregation.

D.A.R.-Daughters of the American Revolution. An organization made up of female descendants of men who fought in the American revolution.

Depression-A time of world wide unemployment (1929-1939.)

G.I.Bill of Rights-A government program to offer World War II veterans college educations and other benefits.

Hitler, Adolf-The German dictator responsible for starting World War II and the Holocaust.

Jim Crow Car-The segregated railroad cars for blacks only. African- Americans were not permitted to ride with whites.

Jim Crow Laws-The laws passed to segregate the black population from the white in public facilities and in schools.

KKK-Klu Klux Klan. A hate group whose goal was to deprive blacks, Jews, Catholics, and "foreigners" of their civil rights.

March on Washington-The march led by Martin Luther King, Jr. August, 1963 to protest segregation and job discrimination.

NAACP-National Association for the Advancement of Colored Peoples-An organization formed to obtain civil rights through the courts.

New Deal-A program created by President Franklin D. Roosevelt to take the United States out of the depression.

OCS-Officers Candidate School. The army schools used to train officers.

Pearl Harbor-The American naval base in Hawaii which was bombed on December 7, 1941 by the Japanese, causing America to enter World War II.

Poor Peoples March-The march on Washington led by the SCLC to demand better living conditions.

Prohibition-The Constitutional amendment forbidding anyone to sell liquor, later repealed.

Queen Mary-The luxury ocean liner converted to a troopship to carry soldiers to Europe during World War II.

Red Ball Express-The truck supply route in Europe that delivered supplies from the ports to the battle lines during World War II. The drivers were African-American soldiers who were members of segregated units.

Resurrection City-The tent camp set up by the Poor People's March on Washington in 1968 to protest lack of employment opportunities.

SCLC-Southern Christian Leadership Conference-The civil rights group formed by the Reverend Martin Luther King, Jr. and Reverend Ralph Abernathy.

SNCC-Student Non-violent Coordinating Committee. An organization that conducted peaceful protests against discrimination.

Urban League-The rights organization formed to help blacks obtain jobs and civil rights.

1

A BUCKET OF BISCUITS

Tilmon heard the first bell ring. Wiping his mouth on his sleeve, he placed the dented molasses bucket behind a rock and, barefooted, ran out of the woods and up the long hill to Browne Junior High School.

Snow, rain, or sunshine, Tilmon always ate his lunch in the woods.

This first day of junior high school, Tilmon pretended that he had forgotten his lunch. He wasn't sure that everyone carried a pail of beaten biscuits and poured molasses to school. He waited to see what the other students brought.

The hungry boy watched as some of the children brought out sandwiches made of store-bought bread wrapped in beautiful, crisp white paper. His mouth watered. Tilmon thought of the sticky lunch his mother had made. How the children would laugh if they saw it!

That night, when his mother came home from work, Tilmon said boldly, "I'd like a peanut butter or a ham sandwich for lunch tomorrow."

His fifteen-year-old brother, Buddy, looked up from his plate of corn bread and black-eyed peas and lisped, "We don't even have that for thupper."

Mama smiled at Tilmon. "I'm doin' the best I can, son. Times is hard. Some folks don't even got no bucket of biscuits and poured molasses for lunch."

Tilmon nodded and never asked again. It was just as easy

11

to leave home a little early each morning. When he came to the woods on Bladensburg Road, Tilmon would slip behind the trees and hide the pail and tin spoon in a hollow stump. Then he would take off his tight-fitting shoes, tie the shoelaces together and sling the shoes over his shoulders. Satisfied that none of his classmates were in sight, he would slip out of the woods and hurry toward school.

The second bell rang.

Tilmon scampered up the steep path leading to Browne, Washington, D. C.'s, newest and finest junior high school for Negroes.

Tilmon ran into the classroom. Dropping a wet frog on the teacher's desk, he dashed into the cloakroom.

Mrs. Scott looked up and watched the slim, honey-colored boy go.

As always, Tilmon pulled a piece of cloth out of his pocket and wiped his feet. Then there was the usual bump, bang, thump as Tilmon backed his shoes against the wall of the cloakroom. Wiggling and twisting, he tried to squeeze his feet into the too-small shoes. Fascinated, the class would listen to Tilmon's twice-daily shoe stomp. Bump, bang, thump. Bump, bang, thump, bump, bump. Somehow, he would kick and twist his feet into the shoes.

Smiling, Tilmon entered the classroom. "Afternoon, Mrs. Scott."

Tilmon walked over to the pencil sharpener. Already, his hands were too big for his body. Homemade cloth suspenders, each of a different color, held up his short, "stovepipe" pants. His tight-fitting flannel shirt was neatly patched at the elbows. His socks, like the suspender straps, did not match. The boy's eyes glowed with mischief.

"Tilmon," said Mrs. Scott as she opened the window to let out the frog, "there are enough frogs in the marshes without you bringing me one every lunch period. Tell your

12

mother to pack you a sandwich. Rainy weather's no time to go home."

"Mama likes me to come to home for lunch," said Tilmon with a smile.

Mrs. Scott began to talk about the large coffee industry in Brazil. Tilmon couldn't pay attention. He kept thinking about his younger brother, Emory. Eleven-year-old Emory had thrown a rock through a store window, and last night the truant officer had paid his mother another visit.

"Mrs. O'Bryant," he said, "if Emory causes one more incident, I shall recommend that he be sent to reform school."

When the man left, Mama asked Emory, "Why is you so evil?"

"I was hungry," Emory answered. Already six feet tall, he never seemed to get enough to eat.

"Bein' hungry ain't no cause for stealin'," said Mama. "Plenty of people walkin' round with empty stomachs. Now fetch me a switch, and I means a big one."

Not even Emory would refuse to bring Mama a switch when she asked for it.

Mama beat Emory until her arm hurt. "My children got to learn right from wrong."

As hard as she tried, Mama still couldn't beat sense into Emory. Trouble seemed to be his second name.

"Tilmon"—Mrs. Scott's voice brought him back to the classroom—"there are two doors and six windows in this classroom. You can go out any one of them, but to come back you have to know how to behave. Now pay attention. There's work to be done."

Tilmon tried to concentrate, but his mind kept drifting back to Emory. It would surely grieve Mama if Emory were sent to reform school. Mama thought she had the best family in all this world.

"Tilmon, Tilmon O'Bryant!" Again, Mrs. Scott's voice

13

brought him back to the classroom. "You are to remain after school."

When the bell rang, Tilmon stayed behind.

"Tilmon," said Mrs. Scott, "I don't understand you. You're a special child. You're one of the brightest boys I've ever met. Why don't you pay attention and learn something? If you don't get an education, you can't go very far."

The boy hung his head. "Yes, ma'am," he nodded.

Tilmon went into the cloakroom and took off his shoes and socks. He tied the shoestrings together and slung them over his shoulders.

As he came out of the classroom, Tilmon saw the janitor mopping the hall. The janitor put down his mop and went into the washroom. To tease him, Tilmon reached out and picked up the mop. Laughing, the boy carried it down the hall.

The janitor came out and saw Tilmon running with his mop. He pretended to be angry. "Stop that, boy! Bring back my mop."

Tilmon laughed and ran faster. He often teased the janitor.

"Just you wait until I get my hands on you," the janitor shouted.

He chased Tilmon down the hall. "You've stolen my mop once too often. I'll give you a whippin' you'll never forget."

Tilmon grinned and ran faster.

"I'm gonna whip you this time, boy," shouted the janitor, coming closer.

Frightened, Tilmon dropped the mop. He dashed into the principal's office. Grabbing Mr. Haynes, the principal, around the legs he shouted, "Save me. Don't let him hit me."

The janitor ran into the office. "Let me have him, Mr. Haynes. Let me have that rascal."

14

Frightened, Tilmon held on tightly to the principal's long legs. "Don't let him get me."

The principal looked at the janitor. The janitor looked at the shaking boy. They all began to laugh.

"Now go on home, child," said Mr. Haynes. "If you put as much energy into studying as you do into teasing, you'll go far."

Tilmon ran out of school, down the hill, and into the woods. He picked up his lunch pail and spoon and headed for home.

2

EMPTY STOMACHS

In 1933 the whole country walked around hungry. Like a smothering blanket, the Great Depression had slipped over the land. Blotting out jobs and paychecks, it pushed the food off the tables of America.

The O'Bryant children always walked around half empty. Even though Mama gave Emory more than the others, he still growled about being hungry.

"Be thankful for what you do got," she would say. "Complainin' don't put no food on the table."

Annie O'Bryant Williams struggled to keep her family of seven children and her senile father fed and clothed. A widow, she had remarried after coming to Washington from South Carolina. Her new husband, Ike Williams, had a job as a railroad worker. He paid the rent, but provided little else.

Mama had to take in laundry as well as go out to work as a domestic. Every morning she awoke at three A.M. From his pallet on the kitchen floor, Tilmon could hear her as she sang "Sweet Hour of Prayer."

Mama would light the potbellied stove, and Tilmon would turn over and go back to sleep as warm air filled the chilly room.

Still singing, Mama made a rackety sound as she rubbed the wash against the scrub board. After she stretched the

1943. A proud Mama poses for her
soldier son

clothes on long wooden benches to dry, Mama baked
biscuits and fixed everyone's lunch.

Out of the house by six, Mama did not return until seven
in the evening.

Slim and tall, Mama twisted her long black hair into a
braid and wrapped it in a bun on the back of her head. Part
Indian and part Negro, Mama always carried herself like a
princess. Tilmon thought she was the prettiest lady he had
ever seen.

"Cousin" Ike, Tilmon's stepfather, kept to himself. Short,
stocky, and silent, he never so much as said hello to his
stepchildren. He even ignored winsome nine-year-old

Molly. Like a mole, he burrowed into his room, coming out only at daybreak. Cousin Ike had a hot plate in the room he shared with Mama. When he came home from work, he would go upstairs and heat a can of Campbell's pork and beans. The aroma would drift downstairs and tease the tongues of the hungry children.

When Cousin Ike was courting Mama, he had given her an Atwater Kent radio. No one else in Ivy City—a small, mostly Negro section of Washington, D. C.—owned one.

Mama always liked to share what little she had. On Sunday evenings the neighbors would drop by after Baptist prayer meetings to listen to President Franklin D. Roosevelt give his famous radio Fireside Chats.

Black men called President Roosevelt "the Great White Father." To a land beside itself with hunger and hopelessness, he promised a New Deal for all people.

During the twenties, many of the men had drifted up from the South and had found employment as janitors and trashmen. Some worked in the railroad yards that sprawled along New York Avenue. Others worked as porters. The women "worked out" as domestics and seamstresses. Mrs. Johnson, who lived across the street from the O'Bryants, still had her job. She sewed mailbags at the post office.

But in 1933 most men sat around, rocking idly on their front porches—no work, no hope. And every day bewildered people found their belongings pushed out onto the sidewalk.

Most of Ivy City was on relief.

Mama often passed the free-soup-and-bread kitchens on her way to work. The lines on Seventh Street, Northwest, would stretch for blocks and blocks. Hungry citizens both black and white, many with burlap tied around their shoes, waited, shamed and silent, for the dole that would help them to survive another day.

Aware of the even more difficult times that other people

18

were experiencing, Annie O'Bryant Williams refused to let her children feel sorry for themselves. "Be thankful for what you do got," she told them.

Deeply religious, Mama always sang her troubles away. With deep gratitude, she thanked the Lord for giving her a husband who provided a roof over their heads.

3

TILMON O'BRYANT IS HIS NAME

Tilmon thought he was dreaming.

He heard his mother scream, "Just you do it! Just you do it!"

Tilmon opened one eye. Mama flew down the stairs. Cousin Ike, his stepfather, raced after her, waving a long, sharp razor.

Terror-stricken, Tilmon jumped up from his pallet. "Garrett, Buddy, Willie Ed," he shouted. "Emory, wake up! Wake up! Cousin Ike is after Mama with a razor."

Garrett jumped up from the couch where he had been sleeping. He rushed over to the steps. Grabbing Ike by the wrists, he pleaded, "Drop it, Cousin Ike."

"Get out of my way," yelled his stepfather, trying to shake loose. "I'm gonna kill your Mama."

Six-foot-four Garrett towered over his short but powerful stepfather. He seized Ike by the wrist. They strained against each other. Years of working on the railroad had given Ike iron muscles. He forced Garrett's hand back. The boy's arm trembled. The sharp blade inched closer. With a tremendous thrust, Garrett pushed it away. Enraged, Ike thrashed out with all his strength and stabbed Garrett's chest.

Stunned, Garrett shoved Ike's hand away. But once again, Cousin Ike overpowered him and plunged the razor into his stepson's chest.

20

Screaming, Mama reached out with her bare hands and seized the sharp edge of the blade. With one furious snap, she broke it in half.

The noise woke Buddy, who slept on a pallet in the kitchen. He grabbed a broom and began to beat Cousin Ike over the head. The broom broke in two. Emory and Tilmon rushed over and pounded their stepfather with their fists. Groaning with pain, Ike dropped to the floor.

Larry and Willie Ed ran upstairs. They threw all of Cousin Ike's belongings into an old satchel and a paper bag. Then Tilmon and Emory carried their stepfather out to the porch. There they dropped him and his possessions and locked the door.

Tilmon looked at Mama. Blood covered the palms of her hands. "I'll fetch the doctor," he said.

"Never you mind," said Mama. "Didn't cut no lifelines. I'll bandage them myself. Go help Garrett."

Just then Garrett noticed that his chest was bleeding. Little Molly ran to get a pot of hot water to clean the wound.

"Cousin Ike better not show his face around here no more," said Garrett.

"No," said Mama. "We'll manage somehow. I'll do the best I can."

The boys began to talk. "We'll hustle," said Willie Ed.

"I can wash cars for a quarter," said Tilmon. "And I'll find me a job."

Buddy laughed bitterly. "Ain't no work to find. Black people are the latht hired and the firtht fired. Grown men thtandin' on the threet corners trying to thell apples or thoelaces. How you gonna find a job?"

"Hush!" said Mama. "Tilmon finishes junior high. He's the smartest in the family. We'll do the best we can."

Mama took another job. After working all day as a

21

domestic, she sewed trousers in a pants factory for twenty-five cents an hour.

Buddy quit school and took a job in a grocery store for eight dollars a week. Garrett was lucky. He already had a job driving a truck for a calculating machine company.

As hard as they all worked, they still couldn't scrape together the twenty-eight dollars necessary to pay the rent.

There was barely enough to put corn bread and black-eyed peas on the table each night. What little money was left went to purchase coal to feed the potbellied stove that warmed the house, heated the laundry water, baked the biscuits, and provided hot water for baths.

Tilmon and Willie would take their wagon and go down to the Sunshine Bakery on Florida Avenue. There they would pick out all the stale bread and cake that the wagon could hold and take it home. These free baked goods, which otherwise would have been carted to the city dump, kept many people in Ivy City alive during the Depression.

Each time the landlord came to collect, the boys would say that Mama wasn't home and that she would bring the money to the office the next day.

One day Tilmon came home from school and found Molly sitting on the steps crying. There was an EVICTION notice tacked on the front door. Two men with marshal's badges were putting all the furniture on the sidewalk.

Tilmon became angry. "What you think you're doing, mister?" he asked, as one of the men dropped the pallets onto the pavement.

The man ignored him.

"Put it back," said Tilmon. "We lives here."

"Not anymore, son," said the marshal. He was tired. This was his fourth eviction that day. "Your folks couldn't pay the rent. You've got to find somewhere else to live."

Tilmon looked around. Pots and pans were scattered all over the tiny lawn. The ironing board leaned against the

Indian cigar tree, and Mama's Sunday dress was stuffed inside the copper-bottomed washtub.

Molly began to bawl louder. Tilmon felt like crying too, but he couldn't see that it would do any good. He shivered. Where would they go? To Shantytown? Folks out there made their own houses of corrugated tin and cut-up pieces of oil drums. The only water came from the outdoor spigot in the middle of the muddy road. A few slapped-together, cold and damp wooden outhouses were shared by hundreds of families. Would they have to build their own house tonight?

It was four o'clock in the afternoon. No one would be home before seven.

"Come on, Molly, it's best we sit inside and wait. We can watch the furniture from there."

The marshal pushed him aside. "We have to board up the house. You don't belong here anymore."

A tear slid down Tilmon's face. He brushed it away.

"Sit on the couch with me, Molly," he said.

Molly climbed on the couch and Tilmon covered her with all the pallets. "We got to watch this furniture 'til Mama and the boys come home."

Mrs. Johnson, who lived across the street, walked over. "You children come and stay with me until your Mama comes home."

"Thank you," said Tilmon, "but we got to watch this furniture for Mama. Don't want nobody stealin' it."

That night, when Mama came around the corner, she saw Molly asleep on the couch and Tilmon watching over her. Her back stiffened. She held her head a little higher than usual. "That's a good child, Tilmon. Run to the place where Garrett works. See if he can borrow a truck. We'll move in with your sister Lillian and her husband. We'll do the best we can."

Fat, jolly Mrs. Johnson came over.

23

"Annie, why don't you let Tilmon stay with us until you get settled?"

"Well," Mama hesitated, "I don't like to tear my family apart."

"Oh, let him stay a few days until you get settled. I'll get him off to school in the morning."

Garrett and Buddy arrived with the borrowed truck. Tilmon helped the boys load the two beds, the radio, a worn flowered rug, the faded-red sofa, pots and pans, dishes, and the carefully mended quilted pallets. It wasn't much, but it was all they had.

When everything was packed, Mama turned to Mrs. Johnson. "Tilmon might as well stay with you. Lord knows what Lillian's husband will say when we all moves in with him."

She gave Tilmon a hug. "Now hold your head up high, son, and don't ever let it down."

Tilmon loved being with the Johnsons. He had a whole bed to himself and clean white sheets. Eddie Johnson helped him with his homework. Tilmon ran errands for Mrs. Johnson and tried to keep the yard and porch neat. Every night there was either chicken or meat for dinner!

But the best part of staying with the Johnsons was his school lunch: two crisply wrapped white bread sandwiches! Tilmon thought he was in heaven.

Sunday morning, Mrs. Johnson woke Tilmon. "Mr. Johnson and I have a present for you."

Surprised, Tilmon opened it. It was a gray, chalk-striped suit! A suit with long trousers! Tilmon had never dreamed of owning a pair of brand-new long pants, and a jacket to match.

He gave each of the Johnsons a hug. "Thank you, thank you, it's the *onliest* present I ever got."

After Tilmon had admired himself in the mirror many times, Mrs. Johnson said, "Time to go to Lillian's. After

24

church, you ask your Mama to come to Sunday dinner. Mr. Johnson and I want to talk to her."

When Tilmon strutted in the door, Mama laughed, "Glory, Tilmon, you're just full of yourself."

Buddy tried on the jacket, but it was too small.

"Gracious, Tilmon." Mama gave him a big hug. "They must feed you good. You done gained a few pounds."

Only Lillian's husband seemed a little grumpy.

"Mama, Mrs. Johnson asked you to Sunday dinner. She'd like to talk to you."

After they had eaten, Mr. Johnson sent Tilmon to the store for some candy.

When he left, Mrs. Johnson said, "Mrs. O'Bryant, we've always wanted a son. We'd like to adopt Tilmon. We love him like he was one of our own."

"Yes," added Mr. Johnson. "If you let us have him, we'll see that he gets a college education. Why, we'll even see him through law school, if that's what he wants."

"Lord a'mighty!" said Mama. "A son of mine a lawyer! Glory be! Lawyer O'Bryant!" and then she stopped and thought a moment. She lifted her chin a little bit higher.

Mama's voice was firm. "I knows you loves my boy. And I knows you would be good to him. But I loves all my children. They was born O'Bryants, and they'll stay O'Bryants. I'll do the best I can. I thank you all kindly, but Tilmon O'Bryant is his name."

When Tilmon came back from the store, his mother said, "Fetch your things. It's time for you to come to home."

4

NOT WILLIE ED

Mama didn't have time to look for a place to live, so Garrett found the white frame house on Montana Avenue. True, it leaned a little, and the steps and porch sagged, as if it were too tired and too old to stand up straight, but it was better than crowding into Lillian's.

As the windows had no shades, every passerby could see inside.

"Go fetch a bucket of whitewash," Mama ordered. "We'll paint the windows. Ain't nobody can see through whitewash."

Everyone hustled, but they still had to go on welfare.

Each time Tilmon had to take the homemade wagon down to the welfare department he wished he were back with the Johnsons. It wasn't the wagon that bothered him. It was the best in Ivy City. He and Willie Ed had made it with parts salvaged from the junk heap.

On the bottom of the wagon Tilmon would always put some newspapers and a brick to hide the government labels on the food bags. It was hard enough being on welfare, you didn't have to tell the whole world.

The two boys never fought about keeping the wagon greased. They needed it for too many things.

The night before the trash men came, Tilmon and Willie Ed would take the wagon and go through all the trash bags in the neighborhood. They could tell by the shape of the burlap bundles whether there were empty milk bottles inside. Storekeepers paid half a cent for each empty, and if the boys were lucky, they would make a dime each on trash days. Then Tilmon and Willie Ed would buy a bottle of pop and a five-cent package of Tasty cupcakes. They would sit on the curb outside Mr. Levy's grocery store and carefully lick the icing off the top of each cupcake. Then slowly, slowly, they would chew the spongy part.

Tilmon also used the wagon to deliver newspapers.

"Extra! Extra!" he would shout when something special happened.

"I declare," said Mrs. Scott, his teacher. "That Tilmon O'Bryant has the loudest voice in Ivy City."

In 1933 most people could not afford two cents a day for a newspaper. When something special happened, the newspapers would put out a five-cent "extra" edition and everyone would try to buy one.

"Extra. Extra! Read all about it!" Tilmon shouted one day. "Prohibition ended. Liquor stores open tomorrow! Happy days are here again! Extra! Extra! Read all about it!"

Everyone rushed up to buy a paper. Everyone tipped Tilmon.

Counting his change, he felt like the richest boy in Ivy City. He had earned two dollars with the "extras."

As he walked past Levy's grocery store, he kicked aside a broken bottle. A group of older men were hanging out in front of the store. A few teen-agers were on their knees shooting craps. Tilmon ignored them. He was trying to decide what to do with his two dollars. Maybe he would surprise everyone and buy a chicken for dinner. He would still have enough left over for some candy and soft drinks. Or maybe he would go to a shoe store and get a pair of shoes that didn't hurt. He would save them for school and Sundays. He liked the sound of the change jingling in his pocket. Maybe he would buy Mama a new dress. Mama was so pretty with her long black hair. She should have nice clothes.

Tilmon waved to the boys crouched over the dice. It was a hard decision trying to figure out what to do with two dollars.

"Hey, Tilmon."

Tilmon looked over at the crap shooters.

His brother Emory called to him from the circle. "Tilmon, lend me fifty cents."

"Ain't got no money to lend you, Emory," Tilmon said softly. He began to walk a little faster.

Emory grabbed Tilmon's arm and twisted his elbow. "I said lend me the money you got sellin' them 'extras.'"

"Aw, let go, Emory. I'm gonna buy a chicken for dinner. Ain't you tired of eatin' black-eyed peas and corn bread?" Tilmon tried to shake loose.

Emory's friend seized Tilmon's other arm. "Come on, lend your brother the money."

They began to empty Tilmon's pockets. Soon they had all his nickels and dimes. Ignoring Tilmon, they went back to shooting dice.

Tilmon shouted furiously, "I hate you, Emory. You ain't nothin' but a pile of trouble." Discouraged, he walked on home. Only Willie Ed was there.

He took one look at Tilmon's face. "What happened?"

"I made two dollars on 'extras,' and Emory took my money." Tilmon didn't know whether to cry or to go upstairs and tear up Emory's things.

"I'm fixin' to go swimmin'," said Willie Ed. "You come on and go with me and Joe. Ain't nothin' we can do 'bout Emory 'cept to go round him. Some people is just born bad."

"I'm gonna steal my money back out of his pocket, just like he steals from Mama," said Tilmon.

28

Willie Ed shrugged. "Emory is bigger and meaner than you. Don't go messin' round with him. He'll kill you. Come on and go swimmin'. Ain't usual to have such a hot day this time of year."

Tilmon shook his head. "I don't feel like it."

Willie Ed slammed the door and went off.

The door slammed again. Cursing, Emory stomped into the house. Tilmon hid behind the couch. He watched Emory go upstairs to Mama's room. Tilmon slipped upstairs. Through the keyhole he watched Emory steal Mama's savings from out of her pillowcase.

Infuriated, Tilmon slipped into the kitchen and picked up the butcher knife. Just as Emory was about to go out of the door, Tilmon jumped him and caught him by surprise. In seconds Emory was down on the floor.

"I'm gonna kill you, Emory. You done caused this family enough grief. Stealin', beatin' people up. We don't need you around here." Tilmon raised the knife.

Just then his oldest sister, Lillian, opened the kitchen door. "Drop that knife, Tilmon! I said, drop that knife. What do you want to do? Kill Emory and Mama at the same time?"

She pulled Tilmon off Emory. "He may be no good, but he's still your brother."

"I'll kill him," said Emory, seizing the butcher knife.

"You will not," said Lillian. "Now, get up and get out of here."

Furious, Emory stomped out of the door.

"Tilmon," said Lillian, "Grandpa's wandered away again. Go find him."

Tilmon walked along, looking in all the stores and barbershops. He met a neighbor coming down the street.

"Lookin' for your grandfather?" the man asked.

"Yes, sir. Did you see him?"

"He's all the way over to Elder Lightfoot's Happy Times Café. Looked like he was enjoyin' himself."

Tilmon became annoyed. The Happy Times Café, which sold food for a penny an item, or gave it away if you had no money, was miles from their house. Tilmon would have to get the wagon and pull Grandpa home.

With a full stomach, Grandpa sang "Happy Am I" all the way home. Tilmon couldn't help laughing and joined in.

Little Molly had black-eyed peas and corn bread ready for supper. Willie Ed hadn't come in yet, but they were too hungry to wait. They sat down to eat.

There was a knock at the door. Willie Ed's friend Joe dashed into the house. "Where's your mama?"

"She's out workin'. Won't be home until seven."

Joe began to sob so hard they could hardly understand him. "Willie Ed—he—Willie Ed, he done drowned! Got caught in a suck hole, and his body just swirled on down." Joe became hysterical. "I just went swimmin' with Willie Ed, and he got sucked on down. Wasn't nothin' I could do."

Molly started to scream. Tilmon just stared at Joe.

"Willie Ed done drowned," said Joe. "Wasn't nothin' I could do. The police are out draggin' for his body."

Tilmon put his arm around Molly. Quiet Willie Ed had been his friend. Willie Ed always let him come fishing. Willie Ed always let him hang around with him and his friends. Willie Ed always listened to his troubles. Why couldn't it have been Emory?

5

HUSTLIN'

Willie Ed hadn't had a job, but he used to hustle after school. Saturday nights he always slipped two or three dollars, earned from running errands and washing cars, into Mama's pillowcase "bank." Tilmon felt that he had to take Willie Ed's place.

One day, after school, he walked into Nat Black's Capitol View Market. "Afternoon, Mr. Black. I'm Mrs. O'Bryant's boy Tilmon. Do you have a job for me? I'd like to help out at home. I can work after school and on Saturdays."

Nat Black looked at the immaculately clean young man in the too-short pants. "I wish I did, but I can't afford help. My wife had to go to work at the navy yard to help support the family."

Tilmon looked dejected.

"Let me call one of my competitors. Perhaps he can use you. Do you have a wagon?"

"The best in Ivy City," Tilmon answered proudly.

Nat Black went to the phone. In a few minutes he was back. "Here's the address," he said, handing Tilmon a piece of paper. "You come back and visit me. You're always welcome."

When he finished working, Tilmon would drop by Nat's store. British-born Nat Black would help him with his grammar and arithmetic, and Tilmon would help unload the canned goods and run errands.

Listening to Nat Black's crisp, precise speech, Tilmon asked, "Whyfor you say 'he doesn't,' Nat, and I say 'he don't'? What difference do it make?"

Nat smiled, pleased that the boy had noticed. "Tilmon, like baseball and football, everything has rules. English grammar is the same way. Foreign-born people and black people have their own grammatical patterns. They understand one another, and there is nothing wrong with their talking that way among themselves. But when a man wants to get a job in an English-speaking world, he has to use the grammar rules of that world. Otherwise, people think he is ignorant. If you can't communicate, you don't get hired.

"It's important for you to know how to express yourself both ways. I'll help you with standard English grammar, but don't you ever look down on the way your mama talks."

Distressed by Tilmon's thinness, Nat Black told Tilmon to help himself to anything in the store or refrigerator.

Tilmon told his mother, "If my daddy were livin', I wish he was just like Nat Black."

The Blacks lived in three tiny rooms above the store. They had a son and two daughters and their quarters were cramped, but not too cramped to keep them from placing a cot in the narrow kitchen for Tilmon. He spent so much of his free time with the Blacks that Nat and Sylvia's relatives began to think of Tilmon as a member of the family—especially Nat's teen-age sisters from New York, who enjoyed teasing him.

The first time they saw Tilmon's newly sprouted mustache, they giggled. Early the next morning the two girls crept into the kitchen. With a sharp razor, they shaved off the right side of the mustache.

When Tilmon awoke and looked in the mirror, he laughed. For weeks he proudly sported half a mustache.

Even though he was at Nat's more than he was at home, Tilmon never forgot his obligations to his mother.

32

On Saturday nights he would hand her four of the five dollars he had earned. One dollar he would keep for "pinch-off" money.

Every Sunday morning, in her round little black straw hat with its red feather and veil, Mama would proudly lead her children to the white frame Bethesda Baptist Church. Her smile covered her whole face, and the little mole on the end of her nose would twitch with pride as each of the O'Bryants stood up on Testament Day and recited in turn,

"I'm not ashamed to own my Lord
Or to defend his cause."

After church Tilmon would go to the Gem Theatre and buy a ticket for ten cents. This admitted him to the "colored" side of the movie house. Munching on a ten-cent bag of "leftover" bakery buns, he would watch the weekly bill, cheering for cowboy Tom Mix, thrilling to the jungle serials of Tarzan, laughing at the Mickey Mouse cartoons, and shivering over the frightening exploits of Frankenstein.

Some Sundays, when the weather was good, the Young People's Union of the Baptist Church would sponsor a straw ride. The price was five cents. A large wagon filled with straw would take twenty-five or thirty teen-agers all around the city of Washington.

Driving down Bladensburg Road, the wagon would roll across the railroad tracks, past the woods, downtown, and around the Washington Monument. Then it would slowly circle the White House with its beautiful gardens. Tilmon always loved the ride down Pennsylvania Avenue, the "Avenue of the Presidents," to the Capitol. Cherry blossom time was the prettiest. The whole city turned into an umbrella of pale-pink flowers.

Whatever money was left over from his "pinch-off" money, Tilmon asked Nat Black to save.

Nat took a small account book and wrote "Tilmon O'Bryant" at the top. Each week he would record the date

33

and the amount. Whatever amount Tilmon gave him, Nat would take and put it in an envelope and place it in a black box.

"Always try to save a little money," Nat said. "Then when you really want or need something, you can get it."

"That's right, Nat. When I'm old enough to get a driver's license, I'm gonna have me a car," Tilmon told him.

One day Freddie Simpkins, an older boy who lived in the neighborhood, approached Tilmon.

"Come on and go with me. I needs your help to pick up some stuff. A few of your buddies is comin'. I'll give you fifty cents."

"Okay," said Tilmon.

Simpkins drove the boys over to the woods in back of the B & O railroad yard. He parked beside a pile of railroad ties and spikes. "You just load this stuff into my truck."

"Are you sure it's all right?" asked Tilmon.

"Sure," said Freddie. "This here is a dump pile. The railroad wants you to clean it up."

"What you gonna do with it?" Tilmon asked.

"Never mind. Just load it on the truck," Simpkins ordered.

The boys lifted the heavy railroad ties into the truck. They had almost filled the back when two policemen came through the woods.

One officer pulled his gun. "Where do you think you're takin' this stuff? It's railroad property. Just unload it."

"Yes, sir," said the boys. Quickly, they replaced the railroad ties and spikes.

Scared, Tilmon wondered what might happen to him. Mama and Nat Black would be mighty disappointed if he went to jail.

"How old are you, son?" the officer asked.

"Fourteen," Tilmon sputtered.

"And you," he asked Freddie.

34

"Eighteen."

"You're under arrest," he told Freddie. "You put the kids up to this. Okay, kids, go on home and stay out of trouble."

Tilmon ran home as fast as he could.

Somehow Mama found out about Tilmon and Freddie Simpkins.

"Fetch me a switch," she told Tilmon, "and make it a mighty big one."

"I didn't know we was stealin', Mama. Freddie said it was all right," Tilmon protested.

"My children got to know right from wrong—for themselves," said Mama, whipping as hard as she could. "Don't you let nobody lead you down-country."

"Stop beatin' me," yelled Tilmon. "You don't give me no chance to do good when you beat so hard."

Mama stopped. "Now you think for yourself. The good Lord done give you a mind of your own. I expect you to use it."

6

THE NICEST CAR IN IVY CITY

Sixteen! Tilmon laughed when Nat handed him a birthday card. It was addressed to "Tilmon Black." Mama had sent it to Nat's store.

On Sundays Nat would pile his wife and children into the car, and they would drive to a restaurant for dinner. They always asked Tilmon to join them. Always, he would refuse.

This time, because it was Tilmon's birthday, they insisted.

He worried all the way there. Didn't the Blacks know a white restaurant wouldn't serve him?

Nat drove to a drive-in owned by a local chain. "Six chicken baskets and six Cokes," he ordered.

The carhop looked inside the car. "I can serve you, but I can't serve *him*."

Nat started the motor. "If you can't serve my guest, you can't serve me."

"Wait a minute, mister," the girl said. "I reckon I kin serve you all out here."

The next day Nat drove him down to the District Building. Tilmon paid the two dollars learner's permit fee. At that time people were allowed to take the road test the same day. Tilmon grinned at Nat as he pulled out three dollars for his driver's license. He couldn't wait to get his own car.

Without telling anyone, he began cutting classes at Armstrong High School.

36

Mama sensed what was happening. She went to see Nat
Black. "Please, Nat, talk to him. I want him to have an
education. Education is like havin' money in the bank. It's
right there, up at the top your head if you ever need it."

Nat spoke to Tilmon. "Give school another year. It's
important to your mother. She never had the opportunity
to go. Do it for her."

Tilmon refused. "Ain't no sense to it for a black man. I
see those Howard University graduates acting as messengers
and clerks. I can drive a truck without sitting through four
years of high school. No, Nat, times are too hard to waste in
school."

That whole year Tilmon worked in the grocery store,
polished cars, and did everything he could to earn money.

One morning he walked into Nat's store. "Nat, how
much money do I have saved?"

Nat took out the account book. "Thirty-five dollars."

"Give it to me. I want to buy Big John's car," Tilmon
demanded.

Nat took off his apron and hung it on a hook. "I'll go look
at it."

"No need to look," argued Tilmon. "I want it and I can
afford it."

Nat insisted on seeing the car.

Big John's car was a broken-down black Ford coupe. The
tires were smooth as hoops.

Nat shook his head. "So you really want a car! Well,
then," he said in his clipped British accent, "I'll take you
over to Northeast Motors on Bladensburg Road. We'll use
the thirty-five dollars for a down payment on a decent car.
I'll cosign the note for you. You understand what cosigning
means, don't you?"

Tilmon shook his head.

"That means that if you miss a payment on the car, I'll
have to make it up for you," explained Nat.

37

"Thank you, Nat," said Tilmon. "You'll never have to make a payment."

That afternoon, Tilmon, proud as a fellow with a new girl, drove up and down Bladensburg Road in his 1935 Ford. He rode all over Ivy City, honking and waving at everyone he saw. They all yelled back as he drove by. It was the nicest car in Ivy City.

"That Tilmon O'Bryant," said Mrs. Scott, his former teacher, "he'll go far."

When Mama saw the car she told him, "You're doin' right well, Tilmon. I'm proud of you. Hold your head up high, son, and don't ever let it down."

Tilmon never missed a payment on the car.

As one of his New Deal measures, President Franklin D. Roosevelt had established a Civilian Conservation Corps, the CCC. His purpose was to take unemployed young men off the streets and train them to do public conservation work. Those who joined the CCC were sent to camps where they learned how to plant trees, build dams, fight forest fires, and erect bridges. The salary, in addition to room and board, was thirty dollars a month. Twenty-two dollars was sent home to the boy's parents.

In 1937, after Emory was sent to reform school, Mrs. O'Bryant decided to enlist Tilmon in the CCC. In addition to keeping him away from the rough crowd that hung around Ivy City, the CCC would provide Mama with a sorely needed monthly income.

A group of Negroes, Tilmon included, were assigned to Camp Chancellorsville near Fredericksburg, Virginia. Nat Black drove him down. Since Tilmon knew how to drive, he was soon given the job of assistant leader and hospital orderly. His duties included chauffeuring the part-time doctor from one camp to another. This promotion paid thirty-eight dollars a month. Tilmon kept ten and the rest was sent to Mama.

One day he decided to teach his buddy, Stacey, to drive. The lesson went fine, until a car approached from the opposite direction. Stacey became frightened and swerved into a ditch.

Tilmon was in a fix! If he admitted that he had had an accident, the camp would not permit him to drive. If he said that Stacey was driving, he would be punished for allowing an unauthorized person to use the car.

Finally, he told the camp commander that he had gone off the road to avoid hitting a cow.

The officer demoted him to private and appointed Stacey to be hospital orderly.

Stacey said nothing, but each month—without being asked—he quietly slipped Tilmon his extra pay.

7

STORM CLOUDS

In 1938 Tilmon returned to Washington. A trained firefighter, he applied to the fire department for a job. The white firemen snickered. The few *black* positions were filled. Tilmon had also learned forestry at the CCC camp, but there were no forests in Ivy City.

Jobs for black men, no matter how well trained, were limited. Tilmon did not even have a high school diploma. Finding a job was difficult.

An acquaintance approached Tilmon. "Hey, man, there's money in sellin' Bibles." He raised his right hand and grinned. "It's the gospel truth. You buy these books from me for two dollars and sell them to other people for twenty-five. Now, ain't that somethin'?"

Tilmon liked the idea of a quick profit. He withdrew fifty dollars from his savings account and bought twenty-five Bibles. Soon he was knocking on doors all over town. "Yes, ma'am, this is the finest Bible you'll ever see." He turned the pages to the pictures. "Ain't no reason to be without one. Two dollars down puts it in your livin' room and a dollar a week keeps it there."

The first two dollars came easy. Getting the rest was not. Each week Tilmon returned to collect another dollar. The shades were always drawn, and no matter how hard he knocked, no one ever answered.

By the end of the month Tilmon decided that the only

40

one who could make money on Bibles was the dude who had sold them to him.

Finally he found a job as a truck driver for a coal company. Six days a week he and his helper bagged, weighed, and delivered eleven tons of sooty coal. Their day started at six A.M. and ended at ten P.M. Some nights it seemed as if he could never scrub off all the layers of coal dust.

Each Saturday night Tilmon found twenty dollars in his pay envelope. When he saw that men who owned their own trucks made thirty-five dollars a week, Tilmon began to save part of his salary. In a short while Tilmon and his brother Buddy bought a truck. Soon they were making more money than black college graduates.

Tilmon felt satisfied. He didn't mind the hard work—he had nothing else to do. And besides, he always liked the jingle of change in his pocket.

He looked around at other Ivy City boys his age. Some were in prison. Others would hold a job only long enough to buy a pint of whiskey or to earn a stake in a crap game.

Tilmon told Mama, "I work too hard for my money to throw it away on 'ignorant oil.' Nat Black started me in to savin' my money, and I ain't fool enough to drink it up."

During the summer Tilmon hauled wood for the Hechinger Lumberyard.

One day a friend said to Tilmon, "Hey, man, how would you like to meet some gals from Miner Teachers College."

Since Washington had a two-school system, Miner trained most of the black teachers.

"Don't mind if I do," said slim-hipped, broad-shouldered Tilmon. A handsome six feet two, he still sported a mustache.

The young men drove up to Mary Magdalene Penn's house at Seventh and Florida Avenue, Northeast. Mary, short and pretty, lived in a house heated by a Latrobe stove.

41

Tilmon marveled over the central heating. Mary's father operated an elevator and her mother worked as a domestic. They could afford to have a nice house and send a daughter to college.

Soon Tilmon was anxious to have Mama meet Mary, but he was ashamed to bring her home. Only two rooms had heat, and there was no electricity—only kerosene lamps. The few pieces of furniture were faded and worn.

He solved the problem by waiting for a summer afternoon. Daylight and warm weather hid the lack of electricity and central heating.

Before long, Mary and Tilmon were going steady. Sometimes they would catch a show at the famous Howard Theatre. Here, in the segregated city, black and white gathered to hear the Negro entertainers. Pearl Bailey was one of the favorites. Boogie-woogie pulsated, bounced, jumped, syncopated, and reverberated through the halls, and Dizzy Gillespie and Thelonius Monk blasted the gospel of "bop" to a rhythm-beating audience.

Mary and Tilmon also enjoyed the movies.

One day *The Washington Star* announced a contest to promote the movie *Abe Lincoln in Illinois*. The man most resembling Lincoln was to receive a twenty-five-dollar savings bond. The winner and his family would also be the guests of the theater at the opening performance.

Hundreds of men sent in their photographs. The Negro community rejoiced when a light-skinned black man won the contest. But their excitement turned to indignation when, because of his color, the winner was not permitted to see the movie!

"I would like to have seen that show," Mary said.

Tilmon shrugged. "There ain't no use thinking about it. No matter how clean or nicely dressed we were, no one would allow us in."

42

"It doesn't make sense," Mary protested. "Lincoln was the Great Emancipator."

"Lots of things don't make sense," Tilmon replied.

In 1939 even Marian Anderson, the great American Negro contralto, had been refused permission to sing in Constitution Hall, the largest auditorium in Washington, D. C. The building was owned by the Daughters of the American Revolution. Despite the fact that black men like Crispus Attucks had died fighting for the American Revolution, the ladies refused to desegregate.

Angered by the DAR's attitude, Harold Ickes, the Secretary of the Interior, telephoned the famous singer. "Miss Anderson, each Easter morning we hold a service on the steps of the Lincoln Memorial. Would you honor us with your performance this year?"

Three o'clock Easter morning, Mama, Mary, and Tilmon climbed into his secondhand truck. Driving downtown, they found the streets dark and still. Only a few stars glistened in the blue-black night sky. The whole world seemed asleep.

Tilmon parked on Constitution Avenue. Hurriedly, they walked toward the Lincoln Memorial. Mary shivered in the chill predawn breeze.

When they reached the end of the reflecting pool, Mama stopped. "Glory be to God! If that ain't a sight for sore eyes."

Spotlights illuminated Abraham Lincoln's seated figure. And in the silent shadows stood more people than Mama had ever seen in her life.

Seventy-five-thousand Americans—black, white, and yellow—had jammed into the streets and parks surrounding the Memorial. In the cold dawn they waited in hushed tribute.

Mama, Mary, and Tilmon squeezed themselves into a space at the end of the Reflecting Pool.

When Miss Anderson finished the "Ave Maria" the vast audience stood silent for a few minutes.

Mama sighed. "Glory be to God! Children, hold your heads up high an' don't ever let them down."

With a feeling of peace, the worshipers left the Lincoln Memorial.

But the spirit of resurrection was soon shattered.

A madman in faraway Germany was threatening to tear apart the world. Screaming that his Germans were a master race, Adolf Hitler boasted that they would seize and then rule the earth, "for a thousand years."

While the world ignored him, Hitler plotted every move. Since 1933, German war factories had churned out guns, tanks, submarines, and superior aircraft. "Fifth columnists," undercover agents, had been planted in enemy countries. Their spying and sabotaging laid the groundwork for the invaders.

The timetable was set. But the world refused to recognize the warnings.

March, 1938: Hitler goose-stepped into Austria. Britain and France watched and were silent.

March, 1939: Hitler surrounded and seized Czechoslovakia. The world opened and then closed its mouth without a protest.

September, 1939: A blitzkrieg, or lightning war, stormed through Poland. Within four weeks, the Poles were swept into the German prize sack.

Suddenly the world woke up. The devil was at its doorstep.

Britain and France declared war on Germany. America began to manufacture guns, ships, and planes.

"Guns Instead of Butter" became the slogan. Washing-machine factories turned to producing bombs. Defense plants operated twenty-four hours a day. War materials were desperately needed for the empty bins of Britain and France as well as for the United States.

For the first time, in 1940, Congress passed a peacetime draft bill. All men between the ages of eighteen and thirty-seven were required to register for the Selective Training and Service Act.

This was just "preparedness." Most people felt that America was safe from invasion. After all, the Atlantic and Pacific Oceans provided natural barriers.

Tilmon shrugged his shoulders and went down to register at his draft board. He told Mary, "If that's the way it's gotta be, that's the way it's gotta be."

Since black men were drafted "according to their percentage of the population," the immediate call-up for Ivy City residents was small.

Washington went about the business of self-defense. Tilmon became a block warden. He was issued a white air-raid helmet and given a course in first aid. If Washington were bombed, the air-raid warden would be in charge of organizing and helping the people on his street.

His brother Larry found a good-paying job as a machinist in the navy yard. The war effort had created jobs. The Depression was fading into history.

The daily war reports grew darker.

The deadly German tarantula moved steadily across Europe, catching more and more countries in its web.

April, 1940: Norway and Denmark captured.

May, 1940: The Netherlands snared.

June, 1940: Belgium and France entrapped.

The roll grew longer and more tragic. The "master race" became more boastful and arrogant.

July, 1940: German bombers began a blitzkrieg over English ports and cities.

August, 1940: The date the German timetable had marked for the downfall of Britain.

45

Only this time, the schedule went awry.

Despite the daily rain of dynamite, British fighter planes climbed into the skies and fought back.

June, 1941: Britain still belonged to the British. The English had made a hole in the spider's web.

Infuriated, Hitler turned his major thrust against his friend, Russia.

Protected by two oceans, the United States watched and remained neutral.

December 7, 1941: Japanese bombers flew across the Pacific Ocean and blasted Pearl Harbor, Hawaii, an American naval base. America was exploded into a war in the Pacific.

The isolationists were confused. Could the country remain neutral in Europe?

Three days later, Germany and Italy declared war on the United States. To paraphrase the words of John Paul Jones, we had just begun to fight.

The fingers of war were reaching out and touching everyone in America. Tilmon knew that he would soon be drafted. He proposed to Mary. The wedding was set for February 7, 1942.

There are no pictures of the groom. Tilmon had not previously tried on his rented tuxedo. Just before the ceremony he discovered that the pants were too short for his long frame. If he pulled the waist up to meet the cummerbund, his white socks showed. If he wore the pants on his hips, his shirt stuck out. Self-conscious, the twenty-one-year-old groom refused to appear in any wedding photographs.

8

THE DREAM

Mary unlocked the mailbox. The letter from the draft board had come. "Tilmon O'Bryant is to report for induction into the Army of the United States on January 1, 1943."

"Well," said Tilmon, "that's the way it's gotta be."

Mary started to cry.

Tilmon put his arms around her. "Don't get upset. You know they don't send colored people to fight. We're only good enough for behind-the-lines labor battalions. All I'll be doing is loadin' trucks."

Despite the protest of civil rights organizations, most Negroes were placed in segregated battalions. These were the "dirty work" units. Black soldiers loaded trucks, laid wire, cleaned beaches, and evacuated the wounded. They also manned the famous "Red Ball Express," a truck supply route that ran through Europe from the ports and beaches to the battle lines. Often, when the vital supplies were delivered, the men of the Red Ball Express grabbed rifles and fought beside their white countrymen. At the Battle of the Bulge, the Red Ball Expressmen helped the 101st Airborne Division in its heavily outnumbered stand against the last great German offensive of the war.

Negroes attended the Army officer candidate school without any problems, but the Air Force established a separate flying school for black cadets. The 99th Pursuit

47

Squadron, under Lt. Col. Benjamin O. Davis, became the first Negro flying unit in the Air Force.

General Douglas MacArthur, in Australia, was one of the few generals willing to accept Negro troops in the combat area. In other theaters of war, several black combat units had to be broken up or placed in service units because of the refusal of many field commanders to integrate.

On New Year's Day, 1943, Tilmon O'Bryant and a group of men from Ivy City were inducted into the Army. A bus took them to Fort Meade, Maryland, to be processed. Tilmon felt comfortable. He knew most of the men and felt that they would be assigned to the same outfit.

The next day on the parade grounds Tilmon was surprised when he heard the sergeant bark out his name. "O'Bryant, step forward!"

Tilmon stepped out of line. "Yes, sir."

"Fort Jackson needs a hospital orderly. Here are your orders. Be on the nine P.M. train to Columbia, South Carolina."

The Jim Crow car, reserved for Negroes, was directly behind the coal engine. All night long the train rocked back and forth belching soot. Tilmon's fresh khaki uniform turned gray. With each mile, he became more anxious. South Carolina was a long way from Washington. What would it be like? Would the men on the base accept him? Would he be going overseas immediately?

Tired and dirty from the twelve-hour ride, Tilmon walked into the white-frame dispensary. The waiting room held a narrow bench, some file cases, and a desk. Behind the desk sat one of the blackest black men that Tilmon had ever seen.

Tilmon saluted. "Private O'Bryant reporting for duty."

The sergeant took a few minutes to inspect Tilmon before answering. "Oh, yes, you're the new orderly. I'll conduct you to your quarters."

48

He led Tilmon down the white hall to a small room crowded with two cots. "You sleep in here with me. Lester is my name." He motioned to the wardrobe against the wall. "Keep your uniform in there. Have you matriculated at a college?"

"Beg your pardon?"

"Did you attend a university or college?" Lester asked.

"No, sir, I only went as far as junior high school," Tilmon replied.

"How is it that they afforded you the opportunity to be a hospital orderly?" the sergeant inquired.

Tilmon put his duffel bag on the floor. "Guess it's 'cause I had experience as a medical orderly in the CCC camp. I know all about hospital routine."

"I am a graduate of a teachers college. I have examined your records. You have an I.Q. of 118. So I anticipate that we shall be able to communicate with each other. I have difficulty finding people of equal intellect to converse with among the rabble stationed here. Most of them cannot read or write."

"Well," said Tilmon, "since you're an educated man and a teacher, maybe you could teach them. We have to help one another."

"I wouldn't waste my energies on that trash," said the black sergeant.

He showed Tilmon the room with the three beds for hospital cases, the pharmacy with its medical supplies, and the examining room. "Your position will be to help administer aid to the doctor during sick call. The rest of the day you will take care of any medical problems that arise. You are to run the Venereal Disease Clinic. Sick call runs from six to eight A.M. The mess hall is across the street. I'll call you in time for chow. You may perform your ablutions now."

"What?" said Tilmon.

49

"Wash up," said the sergeant.

Tilmon learned the hospital routine quickly and was promoted to sergeant. He spent a great deal of his off-duty time reading. He was determined to educate himself further in mathematics, history, and literature. He frequented the base library.

Whenever he was invited into town, he would beg off, saying that he had letters to write.

Many of Tilmon's hours were spent writing letters for men who were illiterate. It disturbed Tilmon that so many of the young soldiers had had no opportunity to attend school.

He spoke to Lester. "You're a teacher. Let's set up a class and teach them to read. A man shouldn't go through life ignorant."

"That trash?" said Lester again. "I wouldn't waste my time."

One Sunday afternoon three men rushed into the infirmary carrying a cook. "Sergeant O'Bryant, Sergeant O'Bryant! The cook's done cut himself!"

Tilmon looked at the deep slash across the man's thigh. Blood spurted down the cook's leg and flowed onto his shoes.

"That's one mean cut," said Tilmon. "Carry him onto the examining table."

He walked over to the supply cabinet, talking to the cook as he picked up an anesthetic. "I'd better fix it. It'd take too long to get a doctor in from town."

Tilmon injected the anesthetic into the man's leg. Carefully, he sewed the inside stitches.

The other men were impressed. "Sergeant O'Bryant, ain't no need for a doctor with you around."

The next morning at sick call the doctor inspected the cook's leg. "Couldn't have sewn it better myself, sergeant. We ought to send you to medical school."

50

The work in the dispensary did not always go so well. Once, at the Venereal Disease Clinic, Tilmon injected the serum into a man's arm. The man began to howl with pain. Tilmon withdrew the needle quickly.

The doctor rushed over. "You only hit part of the vein, sergeant. The rest of the needle went into his arm. Don't get upset. One bad shot out of thousands is a pretty good average. You're the best orderly I have."

Tilmon had been in the Army about five months when Lester rushed into the dispensary. "Hey, have you looked at the bulletin board today?"

"No," said Tilmon. "What's up?"

"We are going to be officers. The notice says that any man with an I.Q. of 110 or over can apply to officer candidate school."

"Pshaw," said Tilmon. "You're dreaming. I can't be an infantry or engineer officer. I don't know enough mathematics."

"You could be a medical administrator," Lester said. "Would you have the effrontery to believe that we could walk around with bars on our shoulders? In a few months, everyone will be saluting us."

Tilmon shook his head. "You're dreaming."

That night Tilmon couldn't sleep. He, Tilmon O'Bryant, the son of a cleaning woman. He, Tilmon O'Bryant, an officer!

Now wouldn't his Mama be proud of him! And Mary— he could see Mary walking beside him down Bennings Road, while everyone stared at those gold bars on his shoulders. Why after the war, he might even make the Army his career. Just think, an Ivy City boy an officer! A boy whose family had once been on relief, working himself up to officer. Lt. Tilmon Bunche O'Bryant, Officer, United States Army!

After sick call the next morning Tilmon approached

51

Lieutenant Short, the dental officer. "Sir, there's a notice on the bulletin board about applying to officer candidate school. I have an I.Q. of 118, so I qualify. Could you help me fill out the application form? I want to be a medical administrator."

"I'd be delighted to help. You're well qualified and a natural leader."

Excitement bubbled inside Tilmon. Each day might bring the notice to report to OCS. Waiting was difficult.

Finally the battalion commander called Tilmon into his office. He was a huge man, with tiny, beady eyes.

Tilmon saluted.

"At ease," the major said. "Sergeant, I understand that you have applied for OCS as a medical administrator."

"Yes, sir," said Tilmon.

The major looked at Tilmon. "I suggest that you apply for infantry or engineer OCS instead."

Tilmon shook his head in disagreement. "Sir, I'm familiar with hospital routines and records. I'd like to be a medical administrator. I'd be fearful I would wash out of engineering or infantry OSC. I only have a junior high school diploma."

The major's beady eyes bored through Tilmon. "I can't approve your application."

"But why, sir?" Tilmon inquired.

The major looked him up and down. After a moment he said, "I don't think a colored man ought to have a clean job. He belongs in a labor battalion. He should have a job where he gets dirty."

Shocked, Tilmon stammered, "Major, you have a quartermaster's insignia on your uniform."

"Salute me, nigger," the major shouted. "And get out of here before I court-martial you for insubordination."

9

DOUBLE CROSS

Like a slavemaster's whip, the words lashed across Tilmon's body. A volcano of frustration and fury swirled inside him, screaming to strike back.

Fists clenched, Tilmon glared at the major. The black bullet eyes grinned, daring Tilmon to hit an officer.

Tilmon forced the boiling volcano to be quiet. Silently he prayed, Lord, let me get out of here without killing that no-account major.

Somehow he turned the knob and found himself in the hall. His stomach churning, Tilmon hurried toward the porch at the other end of the corridor. Nausea swelled in his throat. He had to get outside.

Lieutenant Short had just entered the building.

Pushing him out of the way, Tilmon rushed through the open door. Before he could get down the steps, the vomit erupted. Tilmon leaned over the railing, unable to stop. Tears flowed down his cheeks. Here he was, a grown man, and he could not fight back. His fingers gripped the post. Never in his twenty-one years had he been so humiliated. He retched again.

The lieutenant followed him outside. After a few minutes, he asked softly, " 'Dear John' letter from your wife?"

"No, a kick in the gut from the major."

Short nodded. "A *Southern gentleman.* Let's walk over

Pfc. Tilmon O'Bryant, United States Army
(1944)

to the parade grounds. It's too hot for anyone else to be out there."

Leading Tilmon by the elbow, he turned toward the deserted field. "Now tell me what happened."

Tilmon caught his breath. "Ain't no use for a black man to talk. Black is black. You know what they say, 'If you're white, you're right; if you're black, stay back.' Well, I got kicked back today."

When Short heard the story, he motioned to the flag in the center of the parade grounds. "Tilmon, this is the United States. You've got to protest. You meet me after supper, in front of the enlisted men's mess. I'll borrow a truck and a typewriter. We'll drive out to the firing range and type the letter in the back of the truck."

Shaking his head, Tilmon protested. "I can't write good enough for them fancy West Point generals. If they see a letter from a colored boy, they ain't gonna pay it no mind."

The lieutenant glanced at the flag. It hung listless in the hot still air. "You pledge allegiance to that flag. You have certain rights."

"Well, maybe," Tilmon agreed. "But see here, suppose I tell my buddy about it. He's a schoolteacher. He'll know the proper words."

That evening the three men drove out to the firing range. Sitting in the back of the truck, they carefully worded the letter. Tilmon held the flashlight while Lieutenant Short typed.

When it was finished, he handed Tilmon a carbon copy. "Keep this, and don't let anyone see it."

For several weeks Tilmon heard nothing. It was as he had predicted. The generals were not concerned about a black man's rights.

Hot, dusty July melted into a stickier, muggier August. Tilmon stayed out of the major's way. The unit was preparing to go overseas. Everyone was busy.

One morning the major called Tilmon into his office.

Tilmon entered and saluted. He wondered what was up.

The major's beady eyes bored through Tilmon. "You black bastard! Who do you think you are, writing to the adjutant general?" He shook the paper in Tilmon's perspiring face.

Tilmon acted surprised. "What do you mean, sir?"

The major thrust the letter into Tilmon's hand. "You just read that and tell me that you didn't write it."

Slowly, Tilmon read the letter. Then he looked up. "Beggin' your pardon, sir, but don't you think that language is a little bit biggity for a no-account nigger?"

Snatching the letter out of Tilmon's hand, the major bellowed, "Now look here, boy, is this your name on the end or not?" He shook the paper in Tilmon's face.

"Yes, sir, someone typed my name, but it doesn't have my signature." Tilmon ran his finger over his mustache.

The major's face reddened. The veins around his eyes stood out, ready to pop. "Sergeant O'Bryant, isn't that an accurate report of our conversation?"

"Yes, yes, it is, sir," Tilmon agreed.

"Then you wrote that letter." The major waved it in Tilmon's face.

"Sir, I didn't *sign* that letter." Tilmon wondered how the major could have gotten a copy. He had the only carbon, and that was in his wallet. His buddy had taken the letter to the mailroom. No one else could have known about it.

Sweat dripped from Tilmon's neck and drenched his shirt. He stood at attention, trying not to shiver.

"All right, sergeant," the major said. "I believe you, but take a look at this order."

Tilmon read the paper. "Lieutenant Short is to report for assignment at the port of embarkation, San Francisco."

Handing it back, Tilmon asked, "Why are you showing me this, sir?"

"Because I don't like niggers, and I don't like nigger lovers. You're dismissed! And, darkie, stay out of my way."

Tilmon closed the door. Once again the volcano boiled inside his stomach. It was his fight. Why did the major have to punish Lieutenant Short?

A few days later, a black officer approached Tilmon. He introduced himself as a colonel from the adjutant general's office.

"Man, I didn't know there were any colored colonels. Lieutenant Short was right. This is the United States of America," Tilmon said, pumping his hand up and down.

"I wouldn't be too sure of that, nigger. Why did you go

56

and do a fool thing like reporting the major? It's not going to get you anything but trouble."

Tilmon's smiled disappeared. Here was a black man talking down his nose at him.

"Colonel, my mama told me to hold my head up high and don't ever let it down, and if I don't hold it up high, ain't nobody ever goin' to do it for me. If you've come for the truth, you'll get it. If you're going to be an Uncle Tom, then git."

The colonel hung around for three days and then left.

Finally, orders came through. All leaves were canceled. The unit was scheduled to pull out in a week. Soon they would be in Europe, fighting.

Tilmon thought of Mary. Would he ever see her again? Homesick, he could not even call her. She had no telephone. There was no chance of getting home to say good-by.

On Friday, Tilmon was ordered to report to the major.

Concerned, Tilmon thought about the letter. What had the black colonel recommended to the adjutant general's office?

He knocked at the door.

"Come in, come in," the major called out pleasantly.

Tilmon saluted.

"At ease, sergeant," he said. "Tilmon, I'm not a man to bear grudges. You impress me as a pretty decent guy. How would you like to go home this weekend?"

Tilmon sucked in his breath. "It would be nice, sir, but I know that all leaves are canceled, since we're pulling out this Tuesday."

"No problem, O'Bryant," said the major. "Make out a pass. Have the captain sign it. I'll approve it." He watched Tilmon's surprise turn into excitement.

"Thank you, sir," Tilmon said, saluting. Half dazed, he walked out of the door. What had come over the major?

Maybe the letter to the adjutant general did do some good.

Tilmon half stood, half sat, as the ancient Jim Crow car rocked its smoky way across South Carolina, rumbled through North Carolina, dragged past Virginia, and finally chugged into Union Station, Washington, D. C.

How lucky he was to have gotten this leave!

Coming back, Tilmon blessed the major. That man sure had made up for his nastiness.

Tired, dirty, and exhausted from the long ride, Tilmon headed for his room in the dispensary. He opened the door and shoved in his duffel bag.

Someone was in his bed!

Tilmon shook the man. "Hey, buddy, get out of my bed. I'm dead tired. Ain't no time to fool around."

The sleeper opened one eye. "Ain't your bed, man. You been busted."

"Man, you're crazy," said Tilmon, yanking the soldier onto the floor.

"Let go," yelled the soldier. "You been busted to the rank of private. You is in the labor detachment now. Captain done posted a memo on the bulletin board."

Tilmon couldn't believe it. He rushed down to the office and turned on the lights. He read the sign on the board. "Sergeant O'Bryant has been reduced to the rank of private for the good of the service."

The volcano began to shake and swirl. It tore at his stomach, clutched his throat. Tilmon raced outside and puked.

The next morning Tilmon rushed into the major's office.

"Private O'Bryant," the major shouted. "What's the meaning of your bursting into my office?"

"Major, why did you bust me?" Tilmon demanded.

The major picked up a pencil and began to write. He didn't bother to look at Tilmon. "You know as well as I do, *boy*, that you went home without authorization."

"Major, you and I talked. You told me to go."

The officer picked up the telephone. "O'Bryant, you are the biggest liar I know. You connived and got the captain to sign that pass. Dismissed."

Tilmon stared at the major. The volcano began to churn. He prayed. Please, Lord, let me get out of here without killing that no-account major.

10

A NEW DREAM

Tilmon reported to Sergeant Bierney in the Labor Detachment. Six foot three, and two hundred and twenty pounds of muscle, Sergeant Bierney was a man to fight with and not against.

The black career sergeant barked at Tilmon. "You been transferred to my company. I don't want you to think you're gonna get some soft job just 'cause you can read and write. You gonna work, just like them others." Then he added in a low voice, "I like you, O'Bryant. You're not an Uncle Tom. You're willing to help our people. I seen you writing letters home for them boys and trying to help out in other ways."

Handing Tilmon a clipboard and a list of requisitions, he said, "I need a checker. See that all of this stuff is loaded. We shove off in two days."

Blindly, Tilmon counted the boxes of shovels and picks and mess kits as they were piled onto the trucks. The loaded vehicles pulled out. Empty ones stood waiting. Soon guns, grenades, and ammunition filled these. For two days, Tilmon stood and counted supplies and ached inside.

Everyone had heard about the major's action. They left Tilmon to his misery.

Eighteen thousand troops pushed and crowded aboard the *Queen Mary*. Once the grandest luxury ship afloat, the liner had been stripped of all her fancy furnishings and made into a troopship. Men slept wherever they could find space. Tilmon berthed down in the empty swimming pool. Others snored on the floors of the mirrored dining rooms and gilded ballrooms. The soldiers ate K-rations where once only the finest, most expensive foods had been served.

The ship docked in Glasgow, Scotland. There, the men were herded aboard a train and taken to Cosham, England. It was dark when they arrived. The troops were quartered in a schoolhouse. Few of the tired, homesick men realized that a five-foot wall surrounded the property.

The next morning the men were called out for battalion formation.

The major read the order. "We are all here to assist in the war effort. Unfortunately there are no colored people in England. In order to maintain good relations with the local citizens, I declare the town of Cosham off limits to all colored troops."

As he talked, men were stringing barbed wire around the top of the stone wall.

The major continued. "I have given orders to the guards to 'Shoot to kill' if any of you niggers tries to go over that wire. Company dismissed."

Stunned, Tilmon looked at the other men. Fear and disbelief made everyone silent. Tilmon hurried back to the barracks. He reached for a V-mail letter with a green back. Since all mail was censored by the company commander to prevent the enemy from getting vital information, the Army permitted the men to write one "green letter" a month. This green letter was read by someone outside one's own battalion. A soldier could then feel free to write to his wife or family about personal matters.

Tilmon's green letter did not go to Mary. Instead, he sent it to the Inspector General, Southern Based Sector of the

United States Military Forces, England. He told the Inspector General about the barbed wire and the threat to the Negro troops.

A week later a colonel from the Inspector General's office came to check the camp. He dropped by to talk to Tilmon.

"Why didn't you go through regular channels instead of sending a letter to the Inspector General? You could be court-martialed."

"A black man doesn't have any 'regular' channels," said Tilmon. "I wrote that letter with the full knowledge that I didn't go through channels. I didn't come to fight a war behind barbed wire. Whatever the price I have to pay, I have to pay."

Two days later the barbed wire came down. The major was transferred to another post. Black men were free to go in to town.

D-day plus four. Tilmon's battalion went to France. Every time he passed a dead soldier, he wondered, Why?

From France, the Army battled its way across Europe to Western Germany. The labor battalions followed. Then on May 7, 1945, the killing and the maiming ended. General Jodl, Chief of Staff of the German Army, had signed the surrender agreement at the headquarters of Gen. Dwight D. Eisenhower in Reims, France.

The next day, May 8, President Harry S. Truman declared V-E Day, Victory in Europe Day.

Joyously, everyone celebrated and talked about going home.

But the Army had a problem. If all the experienced troops left, there would be no seasoned men to train the replacements.

A few weeks later a notice appeared on the bulletin board. "Anyone with an I.Q. over 110 who agrees to stay in the Army an additional year will be given a direct commission in the field as a second lieutenant."

Corporal O'Bryant, announcer for the "Hot Rations," an informal group, Giessen, Germany

Tilmon read the announcement. He wanted to get home as quickly as he could. He hadn't seen his family in two years. Still, it would be nice to be a lieutenant. It might be a good idea to make the Army his career. Then Mary could come over and travel with him. They'd see all those geography-book places. Just think, two kids from Ivy City seeing the whole wide world! And he a lieutenant! It was something to consider. The pay was good and the future was secure.

Finally he wrote to Mary. "I have decided to apply for second lieutenant. I think I could make a career of the Army."

A local board, composed of four captains, questioned Tilmon. Impressed, they recommended that he be promoted. Next, he went before a regional board. They also approved. Soon an order came through for Tilmon to report to Heidelberg University. He was to be sworn in as a Second Lieutenant in the United States Army.

The whole Labor Detachment cheered. One of their boys was making it!

The jeep driver woke Tilmon before dawn. "Come on, Mr. Second Lieutenant, we're goin' to Heidelberg."

They drove the two hundred miles to the oldest university in Germany.

Tilmon reported to the administration headquarters and waited. Gradually, the other men who were to be sworn in appeared.

The warrant officer began to call out their names. "Baker, Caufield, Denvers, Ellicott, Jones, Garganza, Holiday, Rozinski, and Wheeler. Report to Room 202 for swearing in."

Tilmon stepped forward. "Excuse me, mister, but you forgot to call my name. It's Corporal O'Bryant."

The short, stocky warrant officer glanced at the list. "Your name's not on it, soldier." He turned away.

"Excuse me, mister, but here is my general order. It says that I'm to report to the University of Heidelberg to be sworn in as a second lieutenant."

"Sorry," said the warrant officer. "Your name is not on the list."

Tilmon became insistent. "Now look here! This general order told me to report today, at Heidelberg University, at two P.M. There must be some mistake. Now who do I see about this? I drove two hundred miles to be sworn in. I'm not leaving until I am."

The warrant officer motioned Tilmon aside. "Corporal, I don't want to get involved. Do you know a Colonel Wilson?"

"Yes, why?"

"He sits on the review board. Now, does that tell you anything? He took your name off the list. Don't quote me, or I'll deny having said it. I don't want to get into any trouble."

"Colonel Wilson!" Tilmon was stunned. "But he can't do a thing like that."

The warrant officer shook his head. "He has, soldier, he has. Now get in your jeep and go back to your post. There's nothing you can do."

Tilmon stood there, unable to move. His driver came up and led him outside. Robot-like, Tilmon allowed himself to be placed in the jeep. For two hundred silent miles Tilmon stared straight ahead, struggling with his fury and frustration. Here he was, humiliated, and he, a grown man, had no way of striking back.

When they arrived at camp, the driver pulled up to the recreation center. Tilmon walked inside. Hundreds of people shouted, "Congratulations."

A huge banner, "Congratulations, Lieutenant O'Bryant," floated across the ceiling. Red, white, and blue crepe-paper streamers fluttered from the rafters. Beautiful dishes filled with sugar-scarce candy and cookies decorated the tables. Everyone was jubilant. One of their boys had made it. They all formed a line. Everyone wanted to shake Tilmon's hand.

Tilmon began to cry.

Everyone hushed.

Tilmon forced himself to speak. "This is one of the most hurtin' things that has ever happened in my life. I didn't get sworn in. Colonel Wilson took my name off the list. I never knew a person could be so cruel."

11

ANYTHING FOR THE VETERAN

The war was over! Everyone was going home! Tilmon and his outfit boarded a Liberty ship and looked forward to the promised "new day" for the returning troops.

The GI Bill of Rights had offered special benefits to all veterans. Anyone who wanted to further his education would have his tuition and part of his expenses paid by the Government. This included on-the-job training programs and college educations. Veterans were to be given preference in job hiring. Government aid was to be extended to them for the purchase of homes.

"Anything for the veterans," was the slogan.

Tilmon soon found out that the slogan should have read, "Anything for the white veterans." The building trades were closed to blacks. Local department stores were not hiring Negroes. The telephone company chose not to give on-the-job training to colored people. Once again, the Capital Transit refused to employ Negroes as platform workers, and a black man who had driven an Army truck through the firing lines was not qualified to drive a bus in the District of Columbia. As before the war, Tilmon found only menial jobs available.

He took a job as a file clerk at the General Accounting Office. For weeks, he filed Government requisition lists, b after a, c after b.

Every day Mary and Tilmon stood in line to take a

streetcar to work. Even before the cars reached their station, they would be crowded with people. The drivers would refuse to halt for more passengers. Often the O'Bryants would have to wait half an hour for an empty streetcar, and they would be late for their jobs.

One snowy day Tilmon said, "Come on, Mary, let's catch the streetcar on the other side and ride it to the end of the line. Then we'll be sure of a seat when it turns around."

Taking Mary by the hand, he crossed over the streetcar tracks.

A shrill whistle blasted their eardrums.

"Jesus Christ!" yelled a black policeman. "What the hell do you think you're doing, you no-account niggers, crossing in the middle of the street? Don't you know there's a law against jaywalking?"

Surprised by the man's vehemence, Tilmon became indignant. "That's no way for a policeman to talk, especially a black policeman."

"Shut your mouth, nigger, or I'll arrest you," ordered the policeman.

Tilmon helped Mary into the streetcar.

For a while he simmered. "It's bad enough to embarrass a grown man in front of his wife, but there's no excuse for using authority poorly. I could be a better policeman than that." Tilmon was silent for a moment. "I'm gonna take the exam for policeman. I'd be a credit both to the department and to the black man."

Not one to waste time, Tilmon went down to the Civil Service Commission on his lunch hour and took the test. The date was December 21, 1945.

Two months later he was notified that he had received a score of 99.

Tilmon could hardly wait until he had his physical. The Army had said that he was in perfect condition. In a few weeks he would be walking his beat.

68

February, March, and April passed. In May, a letter arrived announcing his appointment to the police department. Another letter was to follow concerning his physical examination.

"Are you sure you want to be a policeman?" Mary asked. "They aren't in any hurry to hire you." She was pregnant with their first child and anxious to see him settled.

"I'm gonna sweat them out," said Tilmon. "I'm qualified and I can do the job. No one's going to discourage me. I'll drive a cab until I get on the force."

June and July came and went. It was not until August that the police department remembered to send a letter telling Tilmon to report to the physician's office.

Dressed in his best suit, a clean white shirt, and a plain tie, Tilmon appeared at the medical examiner's. He was the first one there.

The desk sergeant told him to take a seat.

. Tilmon fingered his hat as he sat and waited. He stared at his reflection in his highly polished shoes.

Several white men came in, talked to the desk sergeant and were ushered into the doctor's office. One hour passed. Two hours passed. Tilmon watched the dragging hand of the clock.

The office grew warmer and warmer. The floor fan did little to relieve the heat. Tilmon was afraid to remove his jacket.

At noon the sergeant excused himself and went to lunch.

Hungry, but not daring to leave, Tilmon sat and perspired. He wanted to stand up and walk out, but that was what they wanted. No, he'd sit there all day. He'd sweat them out. He had passed the examination and he was qualified.

The sergeant returned.

Other men entered the doctor's office and left.

Finally, at three P.M. a hungry, tired, and indignant

69

Tilmon O'Bryant was admitted to the doctor's office. His shirt and jacket were as dripping wet as a bathing suit.

The examination was brief.

"Sorry, Tilmon, you failed to meet the standards of the police department."

Tilmon looked the doctor straight in the eye. "The Army said I was in perfect physical condition. What's the trouble?"

"Your tonsils are bad," the doctor replied.

Tilmon buttoned his shirt, picked up his hat and coat, and walked out.

He went directly to his doctor in Ivy City.

"There's nothing wrong with your tonsils, Tilmon," the physician said. "Forget about being a policeman. Don't go where you're not wanted."

Tilmon did not answer.

As soon as he could, he had his tonsils removed at Freedman's Hospital.

When his throat had healed, he appeared at the medical examiner's office. "I'm in perfect physical condition. My tonsils are out."

On September 18, 1946, Michael Tilmon O'Bryant was born.

Tilmon lifted the chubby baby high in the air. "Just you wait and see, your daddy's going to be a policeman. I made up my mind!"

On May 1, 1947, a year and a half after he had passed the written examination, Tilmon was sworn into the police department.

"No wonder there are only forty black policemen on a thousand-man force," said Mary. "There aren't too many Tilmon O'Bryants around."

After attending police training school, the "rookie" cops were asked their precinct preference. Tilmon chose the

His first "beat," Seventh and M Streets,
N.W., Washington, D.C.

busiest one in the city: Number Two, also known as "the wickedest" precinct, because of its high crime rate.

He dropped into the station to learn his assigned beat.

Each patrolman had a partner, and at that time the beats were not integrated.

The head of the precinct, Capt. Clyde Strange, looked at him. "My goodness, I thought you were white. Guess I'll have to reassign you to a black partner. Welcome to the police force."

On his first day Tilmon had to walk the beat by himself. A drunk about five feet tall and weighing less than a hundred pounds crawled into the street. Tilmon blew his whistle and stopped traffic. Casually, he picked the man up by his collar and placed him against a building.

"Aw, leave me alone," the drunk protested. "I'm as steady as the Washington Monument and 'twish' as tall." He began to weave up and down the sidewalk. In a few seconds, the man was crawling on his hands and knees across the intersection.

Tilmon blew his whistle and stopped traffic. Once again he picked the drunk up with one hand and placed him against the side of a store.

"Damn cops," said the drunk. "Won't leave a sober man alone." He stood up and fell flat on his face. "I'm not drunk," he insisted, carefully crawling over to the gutter and almost rolling into a sewer.

Officer O'Bryant scooped him up. It was time to put the man in protective custody. But how? he wondered. If he left the drunk on the sidewalk while he called for a wagon, the man might get hurt. Tiny though he was, the drunk kicked and wiggled too much for Tilmon to carry into the store with him.

Tilmon decided to ask the storekeeper to call a police wagon.

Excited, the storekeeper shouted into the telephone, "There's a policeman in trouble."

In a few minutes, sirens blaring, two precinct cars and a wagon screeched to a stop. Six patrolmen rushed out, nightsticks drawn, ready to help a policeman in distress.

There stood an embarrassed Tilmon holding in one hand a sleepy, pint-sized drunk.

12

NOTHING BUT TROUBLE

One Sunday morning Tilmon was standing in front of the Church of the Immaculate Conception. It was between Masses, and the priest had come outside to chat. A group of white-robed choir boys stood on the steps, trading baseball cards.

Cars pulled up to the curb, unloading the sick and the elderly. At the corner, several people waited for a bus.

The bells chimed nine o'clock.

The priest turned to go inside.

Suddenly gunshots blasted the Sunday-morning stillness. Tilmon glanced across the street. Directly opposite the church, two men stood in the doorway. One man toppled to the ground. The other stood over him, revolver cocked.

"Put down that gun," Tilmon ordered. Slowly, he started to walk across the street.

Pistol pointed, the man watched him approach.

When he reached the killer, Tilmon held out his hand. "I'll take that."

The man handed him the revolver.

"That was a fool thing to do," Captain Strange reprimanded. "Why didn't you shoot first and ask questions later?"

"Captain, if I'd pulled my gun, his first reaction would have been to shoot. This way, I may have saved several lives, his, mine, and some of those people standing around the church."

The captain grumbled.

For five years Tilmon walked his beat. Bustling, busy Seventh Street, Northwest, jumped with the rock 'n' roll music blasting out of the open-door record shops. Elegant furniture stores and shoddy "easy credit" appliance shops flaunted attractive goods beside narrow, crowded tenement houses.

A few blocks away was Washington's Chinatown with its many Oriental restaurants. Hub of the city's furniture center, Seventh Street was always crowded with smartly dressed shoppers, Chinese-American businessmen, hustling street people and raggedy ghetto kids.

"Hey, Officer O'Bryant," a child would call from an open window. "Have you got real bullets in your gun?"

"Sure," Tilman would say, stopping to answer the boy's question.

Noticing everything that happened on the beat and following up on anything unusual, Tilmon earned the respect of storekeepers and street people.

When Officer O'Bryant made a promise, he kept it. The people "in the life," as the underworld was called, would go out of their way to be helpful.

In return, the informer knew that if he got "busted," or arrested, he could call Tilmon, and Officer O'Bryant would ask the detective to "go easy."

Every policeman and detective needs these underworld contacts to help solve crimes. Of course, the names of the informers are kept secret.

Tilmon became friendly with the policeman who patrolled the beat near Mama's apartment. Short, slender Burtell Jefferson had big owllike eyes. Every week, he and "O.B.," as he nicknamed Tilmon, would play pinochle with a group of men.

74

One evening they were playing cards at Jefferson's house. "The Peoples Drug Store at Nineteenth and Pennsylvania Avenue, Northwest, was robbed last night," Oliver Brown mentioned.

"Yea, heard about it," said Jeff, dealing a hand. "The description of the suspect sounded like the nightclub bouncer picked up for assault the other day. Both men weighed over three hundred pounds."

"He'd be a big one to tangle with," Oliver remarked. "But that's not your beat. Your bid, Tilmon."

Tilmon put down his cards. "Come on, Jeff. There can't be too many three-hundred-pound men around. Let's go to headquarters and get his picture and fingerprints."

"Okay, O.B.," Jeff agreed.

"Hey, what about the game?" William Harris called.

"Carry on," Jeff yelled.

The two men hurried down to headquarters. They checked several pages of the police files before they found the picture of the bouncer. They drove up to the drugstore.

"Yes, that's the man." The cashier identified him.

Jeff and Tilmon compared the two sets of fingerprints. They matched!

"That's great," said slender Jeff. "But bringing him in is something else. Three hundred and twenty pounds! And a mean one at that."

Carrying an arrest warrant, Tilmon and Jeff knocked at the man's door.

"Come in," he called.

They opened the door. There stood the suspect, stripped to his waist, lifting two-hundred-pound weights.

Jeff gulped. His owl eyes grew wider.

"Police," Tilmon said, flashing his badge. "We'd like you to come down to headquarters."

Scowling, the suspect put down the weights. "And what if I don't want to?"

"You'll only make it harder on yourself," Tilmon answered.

The bouncer looked at owl-eyed, five-foot-seven Jeff and slender, six-foot-two Tilmon. He laughed.

"Why resist arrest?" Tilmon asked. "It can only go on your record."

"All right," the bouncer agreed. He put on his shirt and went with them.

At the corner of Seventh and O Streets stood the O Street Market. Sawdust covered the floor of the block-long brick building. Huge sides of beef, dangling on hooks from the ceiling, hung next to pink-cheeked pigs. Fish swam around in rusty, four-legged bathtubs, and cheese was cut from hundred-pound wheels. Bushels of red Shenandoah Valley apples, jungle-high stalks of bananas, bunches of green asparagus, and dusty baskets of Maine potatoes crowded the wooden benches, a small part of the harvest of fruits and vegetables.

The smell of freshly baked cakes and newly made candies tickled the noses of everyone who entered the building. Near the door, tall green cans held bright bouquets of flowers. Waiting customers stood three deep behind the stools of the lunch counter, eager to eat the thick slabs of barbecued beef.

The market buzzed with buyers and sellers.

One afternoon a drunk named Willis Peterson pushed his way into the market. Shoving a bushel of potatoes over on the floor, he began to pick a fight with the operator of the stand.

Richard Gadson, a market employee, walked over to the troublemaker. "Look, fella, there's the door. Get out and stay out." He took Peterson by the collar.

Grabbing three meat knives and a cleaver from a butcher

stand, Peterson slashed out. Gadson fell to the floor, blood oozing from the back of his neck.

"I'm gonna kill every one of you," Peterson shouted, thrashing out. The man standing next to him dropped to the ground, his glasses broken, his eye bleeding. Within a few minutes, the berserk Peterson had wounded seven people.

Terrified, everyone poured out of the market onto Seventh Street.

Tilmon and Private Short were patrolling the beat. Hearing the commotion, they drew their guns and rushed inside.

"Drop those knives," Tilmon commanded.

"Get out of here, you goddamn cops, or I'll kill you," Peterson roared.

A few customers cowered in the corners of the market, too frightened to move.

"Put your gun away," Tilmon told Short. "Too many people might get hurt. Use your club."

The two officers moved closer.

"Get back, get back," snarled Peterson.

With a quick thrust, Tilmon knocked the meat cleaver from Peterson's left hand. Ducking to avoid a flying knife, Short beat a second one to the floor.

"Goddamn you cops," Peterson yelled. "I'll kill you."

With his last knife, he slashed out at Short.

Instantly, Tilmon brought his nightstick down on Peterson's head. The man dropped to the floor.

Recommended for the Award of Merit, "for outstanding courage displayed in subduing and placing under arrest a deranged man armed with a cleaver and meat knives who was resisting arrest after having wounded several persons," on January 13, 1950, Privates O'Bryant and Short received Honorable Mention.

77

A white radio dispatcher earned the award "for directing a patrol car to the scene of a crime."

On October 14, 1950, Tilmon's second son, Klevin Edmund O'Bryant, was born.

"This time I'm aimin' for detective," Tilmon whispered to the infant in his arms. "You're gonna be proud of your daddy someday."

After three years, Tilmon was still walking a beat. He wanted desperately to be a detective, but despite several commendations by the Commanding Officer of the Detective Bureau and by the Major and Superintendent of Police for outstanding police work, no one had promoted him.

Tilmon resolved to work harder.

"I swear," said Mary, "you work longer and harder than any other cop I know."

"That's what makes me a good one," Tilman answered.

One day, when Tilmon reported to work, the desk sergeant told him that a complaint had been lodged against him.

"What's the trouble?" asked Tilmon.

"Mr. Rips, who owns a record store over on Bennings Road, Northeast, said you knocked over a record player and smashed fifty or sixty records."

"It couldn't have been me. I've never been in his store."

"Mr. Rips said the man introduced himself as 'Officer O'Bryant.' He fits your description and he was tall and well built. Mr. Rips will be down in a little while."

Tilmon hung around headquarters puzzling over who would have used his name.

"No," said the storekeeper when he saw Tilmon. "The other fellow looked like him, but he was about six feet five and weighed around two hundred and twenty-five pounds. They look enough alike to be brothers. He sure was a mean fellow."

Sick at heart, Tilmon realized who had used his name.

Once again, Emory had caused trouble.

78

13

A THOUSAND DOLLAR BILL

In July, 1952, Tilmon was assigned to duty as a plain-clothesman in the Second Precinct.

He teased Michael, who was starting school. "I told you I'd be a policeman when you were born. And I told Klevin I'd be a detective one day. Now that you're going to school, what shall we aim for?"

"Captain," said short, chubby Michael.

Tilmon laughed. "That's a pretty big dream. There never has been a black captain on the District of Columbia police force. But I'll see what I can do."

Michael was a bright student. Mary had taught him to read, and he was immediately placed in second grade.

After the first day, Michael asked for liverwurst sandwiches for lunch.

"All right," said Mary. "But you never liked liverwurst before."

"I like it now," said Michael, almost ready to cry.

"Don't cry," said Tilmon, remembering his desire to carry a lunch just like the other kids. "Your mother will make you liverwurst sandwiches."

A few days later, Tilmon got off duty at three P.M. He decided to walk toward Michael's school and meet him.

As he turned the corner, he saw Michael being attacked by two eleven-year-old boys. His tiny fists clenched, Michael tried to beat them off.

"We told you to bring two liverwurst sandwiches for lunch, and you only brought one," said the largest boy, holding Michael by the collar.

"I told my mother," said Michael. "But she said that I never even finished one. She gave me an extra piece of fruit."

"We both likes liverwurst sandwiches," said a fat pudgy boy in a T-shirt. "We's gonna turn you around and teach you to bring three of them." He pulled out a switchblade.

Tilmon ran down the street toward Michael. The attackers scattered.

Michael began to cry. "I'm big enough to take care of myself."

"You will be one day," said Tilmon.

That evening Mary and Tilmon discussed the situation at Michael's school.

"There's too rough a crowd there," said Mary. "He's only six years old. Maybe you should try to get him into parochial school. The Catholic church has just ordered their schools to integrate."

"We're not Catholic," said Tilmon. "And I don't know whether we should put him into an all-white school. The kids might not accept him."

"You talk to the priest," said Mary. "See what he says."

The priest was happy to arrange for Michael to attend Holy Name at West Virginia and Neale Avenues, Northeast.

Outgoing Michael had no trouble making friends, and although he was the only black student in his class, he did well.

The parish priest asked Mary and Tilmon to come to school for instruction. A few months later, the O'Bryants became Catholics.

Tilmon found the work as a plainclothesman fascinating. Each case was different.

80

Lower left: Tilmon, Mary, Michael, and Klevin
after conversion to Catholicism

At one time, it was the ambition of every black teen-ager to own a pair of Nettleton loafers. Though this brand of shoes was expensive, every boy felt he had to have a pair.

One day a young man purchased some Nettleton loafers from Rich's Shoe Store on F Street. As he carried his prize home, three boys spotted the shoe box.

"Hey, man," they said. "You is goin' the wrong way. We knows a shortcut."

Forcing the victim into an alley, they took his Nettleton shoes and stripped him of his shirt and pants.

A half hour later, a liquor store was robbed by three boys

carrying a box of shoes and a pair of unwrapped pants and a shirt. The same gang then held up a High's Dairy store. In their haste to get away, they left the pair of stolen trousers on the counter.

Tilmon told Oliver Brown, his partner, "You have to know something about people and their fetishes.

"I know how black kids feel about Nettleton shoes. They keep them highly polished at all times. But only a fellow who has worked hard to pay for a pair of shoes will take care of them. I'm gonna find a guy with beat-up Nettleton loafers, and I'll solve all three cases."

"That's a good theory. How you gonna find that particular pair of shoes in the entire city of Washington?" Oliver asked.

"Most of the kids who get into trouble go to Turner's Arena for dances. We'll go up there on Sunday nights and find the kid with the Nettleton loafers that don't quite fit and that aren't polished."

"You're crazy, O.B.," said Oliver. "But I'll go along with you."

Before he went to Turner's Arena, Tilmon visited Rich's Shoe Store and studied a pair of Nettleton loafers and noted the special details.

From ten P.M. Saturday night to one A.M. on Sunday morning, Tilmon and Oliver stood at the box office and looked down at the feet of each boy who bought tickets. When the box office closed, they walked around the arena, inspecting the shoes of the dancers.

After six dizzying Sunday nights of fancy-footwork-watching, Tilmon tapped a boy on the dance floor. The fellow was wearing ill-fitting Nettleton loafers. The shoes were scuffed and worn at the heels.

The two detectives took the boy to headquarters, where he confessed.

One day Tilmon went around and talked to several of the merchants on Seventh Street. "Kids around here think of a police officer as their enemy. I'd like to raise some money and have the men from the Second Precinct take a couple of busloads of boys to the ball park. Some of those kids have never seen a ball game."

"That's a great idea," Meyer Mazor and the other businessmen agreed. "Just let us know how much you need."

After arranging for the buses and getting tickets from the Senators, Tilmon found that there was enough money left to give each child two dollars to spend as he wished.

One of the white women on the committee wanted to spend the money for the children. "They won't know how to handle two dollars. They'll throw it away. They've never had that much before."

"Miss," said Tilmon, "let's give these children the opportunity, for once in their lives, to do what they please with two dollars. They are used to being told to do this and to do that by the welfare people. Let them make their own decisions for once."

The woman was indignant.

"Do you tell your children how to spend two dollars at the ball park?" asked Tilmon.

"Why, no," she answered.

A happy group of youngsters and police officers boarded the buses at the Second Precinct. The flashboard at the ball park read, "Welcome Kids From the Second Precinct." Newspaper photographers snapped pictures of the group. Everyone cheered the Senators to victory and visited the dressing room afterward.

If there were stomach aches the next day, they were something to brag about.

Ever since he had been a small boy, Mr. Riley had wanted to own a thousand dollar bill.

After years of saving, Mr. Riley walked up to the teller at Riggs Bank one day and spread his paper bag of five, ten, and twenty dollar bills on the counter.

"Hey," he said to the astonished young man. "Lemme have a thousand dollar bill."

Mr. Riley was so proud of his thousand dollar bill that he would go around asking almost anyone, "Hey, man, who got his picture on a thousand dollar bill?"

No one could answer.

So, each time Mr. Riley would reach for his wallet, pull out the thousand dollar bill, and proudly watch the man's eyeballs drop.

"That's him—Mr. Grover Cleveland."

Having shown his thousand dollar bill so often, Mr. Riley knew the serial number by heart.

One day someone picked Mr. Riley's pocket. When he discovered that his wallet was missing, he ran to the police station and gave them the serial number.

The Washington newspapers printed the story with Mr. Riley's picture. The article also stated that "anyone having possession of this particular thousand dollar bill could be charged with grand larceny."

People "in the life" tried to sell the bill for seven hundred and fifty or even five hundred dollars, but the underworld was afraid to buy it.

A few days after the theft, Tilmon received a telephone call.

The man did not identify himself. "People out here 'in the life' say you can be trusted. Can I give you back that bill and no questions asked?"

Tilmon thought about it. He wondered if he would be violating the law. "Call me back in fifteen minutes, and I'll let you know."

Tilmon tried to check with the captain. He couldn't reach him. . . .

In fifteen minutes, the man called back.

Tilmon made the decision. "Okay, no questions asked. Where do I meet you? How will I know you?"

"Meet me at the corner of Fourteenth and Corcoran. I know you. You don't need to know me," the voice said.

Tilmon drove over and waited on the corner.

A well-known bookmaker approached him. "You Mr. O'Bryant?"

"Yes."

"Wait here."

In a few minutes, the man returned with Mr. Riley's thousand dollar bill.

Tilmon thanked him and brought it back to headquarters.

The report read, "Recovered from an unknown subject."

The next day at roll call, the Chief of the Detective Bureau, Ed Scott, asked Tilmon how the man got the bill.

"Chief, I promised not to ask questions. There's the bill, and that's all I know."

14

THE MISSING GLOVE

Probational detective! After six years on the force, Tilmon had been promoted. Now he could be assigned to headquarters and work all over the city. Of course, black detectives were limited to open assignments and duty on either the Vice or Robbery Squads.

"You might as well say," Jeff remarked, "that two thirds of the jobs on the detective force are 'for whites only.' "

In 1952 not one black officer served in the Accident Investigation Unit, the Hack Office, the Fugitive Squad, the Sex Squad, the Check and Fraud Squad, the Homicide Squad, or the Auto Squad.

Determined to be the best detective possible, Tilmon solved more crimes than anyone in his precinct.

When short, round Nunzio Bonaccorsy became head of the Robbery Squad, he called in Tilmon. "O'Bryant, I've been watching you. You've been a policeman twenty-four hours a day. I'm reorganizing the Robbery Squad. I want a bunch of active men who will adhere to my way of thinking, men who have respect for other people. I'd like you to work for me."

Tilmon was pleased. Bonaccorsy was a brilliant detective.

"Okay," said Bonaccorsy, chewing on the stub of his cigar. "You know my motto, 'Treat the person the way you like to be treated, regardless of his race, color, or creed, or if he's the most vicious criminal in the world.' You can be disgusted at a man for what he's done, but there's no reason to blow up at him."

Bonaccorsy also brought Jeff over to the Robbery Squad.

One night a man jumped over the counter of a truck-rental store and held up the cashier. The thief left his palm print on the counter. Several crimes of this type had been committed in the downtown area of Thirteenth Street, Northwest.

An informant called Tilmon. "There's a mean man who comes into the beer garden each night. He's sweet on a girl who works there. He's big and built like a football player. The girl is afraid of him. When the manager let the girl sneak out the back door, this man put a pistol to the manager's head. Said he'd blow his brains out if he let the girl sneak out again. I think the guy just broke out of St. Elizabeth's Hospital."

"Do you know his name?" asked Tilmon.

"No," said the caller. "But he's dangerous. I seen a fellow walk by on the street and accidentally touch him. He pulled his gun and held it to the man's temple."

"Tell me one thing special about him," Tilmon said.

The informer described the man and added, "He wears a red sweater and carries a thirty-eight pulled down on his belt."

Tilmon drove down to the Bureau of Missing Persons at headquarters.

He took the book that listed all the people who had escaped from St. Elizabeth's Mental Hospital. Searching through the two hundred names, he narrowed his hunt down to a six-foot-tall black male, weighing over two hundred pounds. He decided that he was probably a man in his late twenties who had a round face and a dark skin.

Reasoning that if the man had escaped from St. Elizabeth's, he had been arrested before, Tilmon carefully

Mike, Klevin, and Tilmon

examined the photo file. Here, he would find a picture of every person who had been arrested for a criminal offense. On the back of the three-by-five photograph would be a description, the date of arrest, and a fingerprint classification.

Hour after hour, Tilmon looked at every male picture from *A* to *S*. Seven hours later, he blinked at a portrait of a man named Smallwood. The picture showed a young man in his teens. Tilmon checked Smallwood's palm print with the one found on the counter of the truck-rental store. They matched. A current picture of Mr. Smallwood was needed for positive identification. Tilmon hurried to the hospital and obtained the photograph.

When he returned to headquarters, Tilmon said, "Captain, I've found the man."

"He's too dangerous to have running around loose," Bonaccorsy said. "Let's set up a trap. Tilmon, you plan the details."

"Okay, let's put four black detectives in old clothes. They'll go to the beer garden and sit around and have a beer. We'll stake out other teams at the front and back entrances."

Holding a full-scale meeting of all the detectives involved, Tilmon made sure that everyone understood his job.

A white officer, Cahill, who was not involved in the stakeout, listened to the plans.

"Remember," Tilmon instructed. "This is a crazy, vicious criminal. We've got to get him right off. I'm goin' home to get some rest. I'll meet you at eight P.M. Have your shotguns ready. Don't anyone make a move until I meet you."

Tilmon had worked for twenty-four hours straight. He flopped into bed and fell asleep. Fifteen minutes later, the sharp ring of the phone blasted his ears.

"Tilmon"—it was Bonaccorsy—"you'd better come down here. Cahill's been shot, trying to play hero."

"What happened?" Tilmon asked.

"Cahill heard that Smallwood was supposed to be in a certain beer garden. So he went snooping around. When he saw him, he said, 'Is your name Smallwood?' Then Cahill grabbed him from around the back. Smallwood went berserk. He shot Perkoski, Cahill's partner, and then gave it to Cahill. When they chased Smallwood, he ran down an alley, kicked open a window, and dived inside, only to find himself in a boarded-up closet. When the police dogs started barking, Smallwood shot himself."

The police department rewarded Detective Cahill's "bravery" by giving him the Policeman of the Month award.

Bonaccorsy grumbled, "They shoulda reprimanded him

89

for disobeying orders. O'Bryant identified Smallwood. Cahill loused up O'Bryant's planning and took credit for another man's work. The fool could have gotten killed."

A few days later Bonaccorsy sent Tilmon into the area of the South Capitol Parkway. At least a dozen women had been attacked and robbed. The community demanded protection.

"Go over there and see what you can find," he told Tilmon.

Several of the women had been jumped as they walked up a wooded hill leading to some apartments. Under one of the bushes, Tilmon found a brown, fur-lined glove. He returned to headquarters.

"I'm gonna put this glove on the guy's hand one day," Tilmon boasted.

"Hmph," grunted Bonaccorsy. "Which day?"

"Before I go off duty," Tilmon grinned.

A few days before, the Sex Squad had picked up two boys who a woman claimed had attempted to molest her. The Sex Squad questioned the boys and then let them go.

Captain Bonaccorsy was furious. "Look what they done. The kids picked on this lady, and the Sex Squad let them go. Go look into the boys' backgrounds."

One of the boys lived with his grandmother in a housing development.

Wearing a T-shirt and work pants, Tilmon went to the boy's house. His grandmother was sitting on the porch.

"Where's Newman?" Tilmon asked, like he was one of the gang.

"Upstairs," said the grandmother.

Tilmon went up and knocked on the door.

"Come on in," yelled Newman.

"I'm Officer O'Bryant. I want to talk to you." Tilmon sat down on the boy's bed. He glanced at the open closet. "Man, you got some good-looking clothes."

90

On the top shelf was an open box filled with wrist-watches, lipsticks, fountain pens, and jewelry.

Tilmon walked over and took down the box. "Who's stuff?"

"I got a lot of broads, they give me stuff," Newman answered.

"H'mmm, they wear some fancy jewelry," Tilmon placed the box on the bed and casually ran his hand through it. A brown fur-lined glove fell out. At the bottom of the box Tilmon felt two little books. He pulled them loose. They were Catholic missals.

"Man, I didn't know you were Catholic," said Tilmon.

"They belong to one of my girl friends," Newman mumbled.

A religious card dropped out of one of the missals. On the back of the card was the name of one of the victims.

"Come on down to headquarters," said Tilmon, pocketing the glove and the religious card.

"What for, man, I ain't done nothin'," Newman protested.

"If you ain't done nothin', there's nothin' to be afraid of. Now, come on down."

"Man, I ain't goin'. You ain't got no right to come in here." Newman looked around for something to defend himself with.

"We'd better sit down and talk," said Tilmon. "I know more about you than you think I do. You can lie to me if you like, but I'm not the person you have to deal with. This victim"—Tilmon waved the missal at Newman—"she's the one who holds your fate. If she tells the judge to be lenient, it's better than me saying you weren't cooperative."

Newman sat rigid on the bed.

"You're goin' to jail, no question about that. I have the case locked up. All that has to be decided is whether it's to be for one year or twenty. There's a big difference."

Knowing that an apology was a confession, Tilmon added, "You'd better apologize to that lady. It'd go a lot easier if you do."

"All right," the boy agreed.

Early the next morning Tilmon placed the missing glove on Bonaccorsy's desk.

"What took you so long, O'Bryant?" the captain asked. "You had to work overtime. Give me the details on our way over to the Sex Squad. I always like to solve their cases for them."

Bonaccorsy nominated Tilmon for the Policeman of the Month award, "for displaying a marked degree of initiative, zeal, and investigative ability . . . and skillful interrogation and effective police action."

But once again, the authorities decided that Honorable Mention would do.

Bonaccorsy spit. "Baloney! That's what you get for being the most outstanding detective on the force."

15

IF YOU'RE BLACK, STAY BACK

Tilmon was hopping mad, but he tried to hold in his anger. The list of police promotions had just been posted. The names of O'Bryant and Jefferson were missing.

Jeff walked into the locker room and read Tilmon's face. "Come on, we're early. Let's get some coffee."

Once outside, Tilmon exploded. "Not only were we not included, but some pretty poor white choices got promoted ahead of us, and without even taking the police exams. As hard as we work, and after ten years, we're still probational detectives."

Jeff agreed. "It's enough to make you turn around and quit."

"No, that's what the police department wants. They'd like every black man to get disgusted and resign. Then they could say that blacks don't want to be policemen."

They walked into the drugstore and ordered coffee.

Pushing the sugar bowl toward Tilmon, Jeff said, "Looks like there's enough sugar to wash down your coffee."

Tilmon had to laugh. "I might even save you a spoonful or two."

Placing four heaping spoons of sugar in his coffee, Tilmon stirred it thoughtfully. "We've got to destroy the myth that it's no use for a black man to try. We've got to study and challenge the system."

Jeff sipped his coffee. "But there are just two of us.

Suppose we fail? Say, why don't we organize a study course? Then a bunch of guys could study together and help one another. Some of us would be bound to pass."

"Pard, you just got yourself a deal," Tilmon said. "The two of us can take the regulations, the police manual, and the codes and divide them into weekly lessons."

"We'll figure out every possible question," Jeff agreed. "We'll beat them at their own game."

Tilmon laughed. "If we start getting too many promotions, and they say, 'You've got to run up and down the steps of the Washington Monument before you get promoted,' then I'll say, 'Let's practice running.' Just make sure the white guys don't start halfway up."

Utilizing tape recordings, the two men prepared the study plan. Strict rules were established. The classes were to meet twice a week from April to October. No one was permitted to leave the four-hour sessions. If a member missed more than two classes, he was expelled. No beer was allowed, only soft drinks. Tilmon was afraid that if beer cans were found in Jeff's trash basket, then the class would be accused of being a drinking party.

When he addressed the nine members of the class, Tilmon said, "Our object is to wipe fear out of your minds. If you study and absorb what you are taught, you will be promoted. A passing grade guarantees a promotion."

On the day the exam results were posted, the O'Bryant and Jefferson families celebrated. Eight of the nine members had passed. Black men had proven that they could pass the police examinations and win promotion *on merit.*

One evening, three black teen-agers walked into the Chipps Grill, a "white" bar on Eleventh Street, Northwest, and ordered beer.

The Supreme Court had recently ruled that all restau-

94

rants in Washington must serve everyone regardless of color.

"I ain't gonna serve no niggers," Edith Barkley, the waitress, exclaimed.

Furious, one of the boys slapped her in the face.

The two others opened the cash register and made off with forty-eight dollars.

Within half an hour, the whole Second Precinct was surrounded by policemen and plainclothesmen. Mrs. Barkley could only describe the boys as being colored teen-agers around seventeen or eighteen years old.

In four hours, the police had dragged down to headquarters every black teen-ager who walked out of a store, a movie house, or even strolled down the street. Over one hundred youths were locked up "for investigative arrest" and kept overnight. None of those arrested were permitted to call their parents.

The next morning the young men were paraded before Mrs. Barkley in the police lineup. She could not identify any of them.

Tilmon boiled. Now all these young men had arrest records. No one had bothered to talk to them on the streets before apprehending them.

During all the commotion, Tilmon had heard a nine-year-old girl remark to her friend, "I knew them boys was gonna' do somethin' bad when they went in that place. They was evil lookin'."

Tilmon found out the child's name. After receiving permission from her aunt, he questioned the girl.

"I don't know their names, but I know where one of them lives. On N Street."

"Fine," Tilmon said. "When it's dark, I'll drive you over there. You can point out the house, and no one will know that you helped me."

A family with five teen-age boys lived in the house.

95

Checking the police files, Tilmon pulled pictures of each of the boys.

"That's him, the one with the scar on his cheek," the little girl told Tilmon. "He's the one I seen goin' into the beer garden."

When the boy left his home, Tilmon followed him to Seventh Street.

"Hey, man," he called from his unmarked car. "I'd like to talk to you."

The boy came over. "What you want, man? I ain't got no time to jaw."

Tilmon pulled out his identification. "Get in the car."

The boy protested. "Man, I ain't done nothin'."

"If you ain't done nothin', then you ain't got nothin' to be scared of."

In a short while, Tilmon had the confession.

An article in *The Washington Post* praised "a brilliant young detective who arrested the people responsible for the crime. None of these boys was among the one hundred and ten youngsters unlawfully arrested on the night of the crime."

As a result of Tilmon's detective work and the efforts of Edward Bennett Williams, a prominent attorney, unlawful arrests were abolished by order of the District of Columbia Commissioners.

In 1959 Tilmon and Jeff organized a second police examination review course. Eleven out of eleven classmates were promoted. It was time for Tilmon and Jeff to receive sergeant's stripes.

The day the list of promotions came out, Tilmon reported to work early. Rushing over to the bulletin board, he searched for his name.

Once again, "O'Bryant" was missing.

Tilmon felt his insides twisting and turning.

Last week, Captain Bonaccorsy had assured him that he had made sergeant. Bonaccorsy was a straight shooter. What had happened?

He hurried down the hall to the captain's office. Today was the last day that changes could be made. Tomorrow would be too late.

It was Bonaccorsy's day off.

Tilmon slumped down on a bench. As hard as he had worked as a detective . . . and getting the highest grade on the exam . . . and then to get slapped down. . . . Maybe he should quit.

Captain Bonaccorsy walked into the station. "O'Bryant, come into my office."

He closed the door.

Tilmon took a chair.

"I've just been down to headquarters to find out why someone took your name off the list of promotions," the chubby captain said.

"It's not the first time that's happened," Tilmon said bitterly.

"Well, the chief was on vacation. So I called him long-distance. He said to put your name back on the list; and you know what happened? That no-good deputy refused. Just refused an order from the chief! How do you like that baloney?"

Tilmon felt sick. As hard as he had worked, and one bigoted deputy was depriving him of his promotion.

Bonaccorsy continued. "So I called the chief again. And he said that if the deputy wouldn't do it, to do it myself. So I did."

He pulled out a promotion sheet. "Congratulations, Detective Sergeant O'Bryant."

"Thanks," said Tilmon, "I know I have at least one friend in the police department."

16

ON THE MARCH

Michael, Klevin, and Mary heard the car drive up. The boys rushed out the door shouting, "Hi, sarge!"

"We just heard the news of your promotion on the radio," Mary said. "We're all so proud of you." Then she frowned, "but I suppose this will make you work even harder."

Tilmon ran his index finger over his mustache. "Mary, I'm a policeman. A policeman is on call twenty-four hours a day, especially when he's on the Robbery Squad. There's been a whole series of holdups around Seventh Street, and not one of them has been solved. I'm going to poke around and see what I can find."

Biting her lip, Mary kept herself from crying. "But that's not your case—let someone else do it."

Tilmon studied the reports on the Seventh Street robberies. In one, a young thug had walked into a small grocery store. Placing a gun against the proprietor's ear, he had said, "Okay, Pop, hand over your cash, or I'll blow your brains out."

Trembling, the old man had opened the register.

When the holdup man left, the grocer had called the police. "Help! I've been robbed . . . Description? . . . I know it's foolish, but all I can remember . . . he had beautiful eyes."

"How do you like that?" the desk sergeant asked Tilmon. "Now we're running a beauty contest. All the victims described the holdup guy as having 'beautiful eyes.' Find the eyes, find the guy."

"I once found a pair of shoes," Tilmon answered. "I can find eyes!"

The thief had dropped his hat in one of the robberies. The initials S. S. on the inside band provided the only other clue.

Meticulously checking the S section of the police files, Tilmon narrowed the initials S. S. to a possible suspect, Sam Smith. The photograph showed a teen-age boy with beautiful black eyes.

Sam Smith had been in and out of foster homes. His last foster mother was working at Ann's Hot Dog Stand on U Street.

Tilmon waited until she finished work.

"I ain't seen Sam for quite a spell. He used to hang with Poo Dog," she said when questioned about his friends.

"Poo Dog?" Tilmon asked. "What does he look like?"

"He has squinchy eyes. He's a Ko-rean-lookin' Negro. I seen him by Mama's Carry-Out Shop on Fourteenth Street."

"Tell me something special about Sam Smith."

"Sam's eyes is just like a beaver's. Bright and shiny as they can be. I used to marvel at his eyes."

There were over a quarter of a million pictures on file at headquarters. Tilmon took a deep breath and began with the A's. Looking for a Negro with Korean features, he searched every photograph. When he came to a picture marked Alston, he flipped it over. Poo Dog was written on the back.

"You're gettin slow, O'Bryant," Bonaccorsy joked. "You've been on this case for a day and haven't cracked it yet."

"I will, Captain, before I go home."

At midnight Tilmon took Sergeant Mathew Bailey and

Sergeant Shirley O'Neill with him. They went to the red-brick tenement where Poo Dog had a room. Bailey went around to cover the back.

Knocking on the front door, Tilmon woke up the landlady. "Is Alston here?"

She opened the door a crack. "Who are you?"

"Police."

"No, he moved three months ago," she replied. A single bare bulb in the hallway revealed a stout lady with pink curlers in her hair.

"Who lives there now?" Tilmon stepped inside the narrow hallway.

"Sam Smith. Top of the steps, first room on the right."

Tilmon bounded up the uneven wooden steps. He knocked at the door.

"Who is it?" a sleepy voice called out.

"Poo Dog," Tilmon answered.

Sam Smith unlocked the door. Grabbing him by the arm, Tilmon shone a flashlight in his face.

"This is the guy," he called to the two other detectives. "His eyes are just like marbles."

The next morning Bonaccorsy called in Tilmon. "Congratulations. You've led the Robbery Squad in the number of closed cases. If you pass the next exam, I wouldn't be surprised if you made lieutenant."

Several months later, Tilmon and Jeff set up their third police examination review course. This time, white officers asked to be included. Jeff's basement could not hold all the students, so they met in the Holy Name Catholic Church.

Everything appeared to go smoothly. Jeff and Tilmon were experienced instructors. The class was full of promise and hope. From one colored officer in 1957, Corporal Ruffin, there were now, in 1963, several black men with the rank of sergeant and two black lieutenants. Nothing could hold them back.

100

One morning, when Tilmon was driving down Fourteenth Street, a man in a yellow Cadillac blew his horn and motioned for Tilmon to pull over to the curb.

Recognizing him as a man "in the life," Tilmon parked his car and waited. The yellow Cadillac pulled up in back and the driver walked over. Dressed in a black-and-white houndstooth suit and a flowery tie, the "hustler" showed yellow shirt-sleeves glistening with diamond cuff links.

"Hear you've been studyin', O'Bryant," he paused and rolled a toothpick around in the corner of his mouth. He looked up and down the street. "We're proud of you. Ain't too many black officers." He paused and spit out the toothpick. "But be careful! You is bein' watched."

"How do you know?" Tilmon asked.

"Got eyes," he answered and walked away.

Tilmon shook his head. Here they were, on two different sides of the law, and that "brother" had gone out of his way to warn Tilmon.

The next evening, Tilmon called for a break in the middle of the session, and contrary to the rules, said, "I'm just going around the corner for an ice-cream cone. I'll be right back."

Across the street from the church Tilmon spotted a car with two detectives. So the department was still trying to discredit the study course! It was hard to understand. Here he was doing his best to improve the quality of officers, and instead of commending and helping him, the top command was trying to find an excuse for stopping the classes. They were really afraid of the black man getting ahead on merit.

Tilmon bought a double-dip strawberry ice cream cone. Slowly eating it, he walked back to the church. The car was still there.

Before Tilmon dismissed the class that evening, he looked out of the window. The detectives had not moved.

The following night Tilmon checked again. His "guardians" were still watching.

Halfway through the session, he called a break and went out for another ice-cream cone. Crossing the street, he greeted the detectives. "Hi, how are things?"

"Fine," the surprised men answered.

They chatted a while, and then Tilmon said, "Got to get back to my class. Like to sit in?"

"No," one of the men answered, "we have to get home."

Tilmon returned to class and the two detectives drove off.

Once again the members of the class were successful. Tilmon was promoted to lieutenant and placed in charge of all the detectives in the Second Precinct. He became the first Negro to be given command of a precinct detective force.

Tilmon's years in Number Two were exciting ones.

All over the country, black men were standing up and demonstrating for their constitutional and moral rights. Led by the Reverend Martin Luther King, Jr., they boycotted segregated buses, "sat-in" in "whites only" restaurants, and picketed business for equal job opportunities. Throughout the South, Negro voter-registration parade drives met with high-pressure water hoses, police dogs, and jail sentences. But the new spirit refused to bow down and be snuffed out. The black man had taken his history into his own hands. He was prepared to stand up and die for his rights.

In August of 1963, two hundred and fifty thousand people, both black and white, met in Washington. With Dr. King at their head, they marched together to the front of the Lincoln Memorial.

The police department prepared for trouble. There were threats against Dr. King's life. Tilmon and Jeff were detailed to guard him.

Waving banners—"Freedom Now," "Jobs and Free-

Lt. Tilmon O'Bryant guarding Martin Luther
King, Jr., during President Kennedy's funeral

dom," and "We March for Integrated Schools"—the huge but orderly crowd surged closer and closer to the beloved Dr. King. Everyone wanted to get as near to his idol as possible. Apprehensive, Tilmon and Jeff carefully watched the crowd, but there was no sign of hostility or danger. Dr. King was safe in Washington.

Three months later, Dr. King returned to Washington on a sadder mission. On November 22, 1963, an assassin's bullet had blasted away the life of the thirty-fifth President of the United States, John F. Kennedy.

Again, Tilmon was detailed to guard Dr. King. He stayed with him throughout the funeral and accompanied him when he paid his respects to the President's family.

The black community mourned Kennedy's death. The President had thrown his moral and executive support behind the decisions of the Supreme Court. He had given new hope to the black man.

The black man in Washington, as in other cities, had begun to stand up for his rights. Where formerly one white policeman could control a hundred blacks, now many white officers had to be deployed to deal with even small disturbances. There was always the threat of a riot.

"Authority is no excuse for brutality," Tilmon told his detectives. "Policemen are servants of the community. 'Cool it,' and we can handle any situation. We are here to help people, not rile them."

Stocky, red-wigged Louise Jackson, a resident of Ninth Street, agreed with him. She organized the first Police and Community Relations Advisory Group in Washington. A natural leader, she wanted to "get everyone together" to talk about the problems that the citizens were having with the police.

Starting with a committee of five, she built her troubleshooting group to over one hundred and fifty neighborhood members. If there was a rumor of police brutality,

104

Mrs. Jackson, or one of her committee, would go out into the streets and inquire, "Do you know this to be a fact? We're all upset. I'm goin' to get some facts. Hold everything tight 'til I get back."

Knowing Tilmon's reputation for honesty and fairness, she would come to him. "Man, I got to tell the people out there somethin'. Give me facts."

Tilmon would investigate each matter. If the rumor was false, he provided proof. If the police were wrong, he said so.

On these occasions, Mrs. Jackson would tell the group, "Man, the police was wrong. I got it from the horse's mouth. You waited for me this long. Let's get together and go downtown to the Mayor and see what can be done."

After the 1965 riots in Los Angeles and Newark, Mrs. Jackson said to Tilmon, "It's a good thing I got a strong mind to try and organize people in the right way. Long as we can talk and check the facts, we can control trouble. Ain't nothin' but black people hurt when there's a riot. Most of the merchants has insurance, but the people livin' on top of the stores—they get burned out. What the department needs is understandin' people at the top like you."

Again it was time for another police examination review course, and Tilmon could almost feel those captain's bars on his sleeve. This was the fourth class that he and Jeff had conducted, and everything was going smoothly.

Midway through the course there was notice for Tilmon to report to Chief Layton.

"O'Bryant," the slim, erect chief said. "You've been an outstanding policeman. How would you like to attend the FBI Academy?"

Tilmon swallowed. "FBI Academy? Sir, that's the 'West Point of Law Enforcement.' It's an honor to be asked to participate."

105

Capt. Tilmon O'Bryant, two ladies from the Community Volunteer Aids, and Mayor Walter Washington

"Yes, it is. We've submitted your name. You have all the qualifications. You have an outstanding reputation and you're in top physical shape. In short, you sum up the FBI's guidelines for members of the National Academy, 'Be a Gentleman!' How would you like to represent the Metropolitan Police Department this session?"

"May I think about it, sir?" Tilmon pressed his index finger against his nose.

"Let me know tomorrow. The course starts next week and you have to have an FBI clearance."

"Well," Jeff whistled when he heard the news. "You'd be the first black man to attend the FBI Academy. Why didn't you say yes?"

Tilmon rubbed his index finger against the side of his nose. "Going to the Academy would take all my time. I wouldn't be able to finish conducting the review course. I wouldn't even have time to study. It's a choice between the Academy and making captain."

"When it knocks, man, take it," Jeff replied.

"You're right, I'll take it as it comes."

A few days later, an annoyed Chief Layton called Tilmon down to headquarters. "O'Bryant, the FBI wants to reject your application."

"Why, sir?"

"You don't have a high school diploma. The FBI won't waive that requirement. You'll have to take the high school equivalency test tomorrow. I've made all the arrangements."

"But I won't have time to brush up," Tilmon protested.

Worried about passing, Tilmon found it hard to concentrate on the examination. He sweated as he answered each question. It had been a long time since Browne Junior High.

Two days later, Chief Layton called. "Congratulations, O'Bryant. You're a member of the seventy-sixth National Academy class."

17

NO PLACE TO GO BUT UP

Trying to appear relaxed, Tilmon listened to Jim Cotter, the National Academy supervisor, welcome the seventy-sixth class. He glanced around the room. The students came from every state in the union, as well as from several foreign countries. They ranged from police chiefs to privates.

How would these men react toward him? Would the Southern officers try to make him uncomfortable? Would everyone be watching him, waiting for him to fail?

His left hand tightened into a fist. Each knuckle stood out. He had to make good. He had to show the police department and the FBI that a black man had the intelligence to attend the National Academy.

Trim, balding Jim Cotter discussed the course. "A drop of blood, one hair, a footprint can solve a crime. In the FBI laboratory, you will learn how to use science to solve cases. You will also learn how to take this evidence and prepare a case. At the end of twelve weeks, you will be experts in police management and administration. When you return home, you are expected to teach these methods to the other men on your force."

Some of the men groaned.

Jim smiled. "Our course in education and public speaking will help you. Apply yourself and keep good notes"—he gestured toward the black notebook on each desk—"and you'll have no problems."

Two weeks of the course were held at the FBI Special Agents School at Quantico, Virginia. Covering eighty acres, the grounds contained a barracks, classrooms, and a large outdoor firing range. Every day the Blue Academy buses took the men from the barracks to the target-practice area. Before going to the range, they entered a large hall. Here they found one wall covered with pistols. Beneath each pistol was its name and behind each pistol was its picture.

"Okay, gentlemen," said "Big George" Zeiss, a bear of a man. "Pick up a pistol. When we're finished with practice, bring it back and hang it in its proper place. If you put the pistol in the wrong place, we'll check the fingerprints and catch you."

Everyone laughed and followed him outside. The large green firing range was immaculate. Huge underground vaults held the ammunition. Concrete walkways led to towers with loudspeakers. Here sat some of the instructors, barking down directions.

The officers lined up to practice shooting at life-sized paper figures.

With patience and humor, Big George Zeiss and the other instructors helped every man improve his shooting.

Riot control was also part of the Quantico curriculum. Using moving pictures, the FBI showed how past demonstrations had been handled.

When civil rights protestors locked arms together and sat down in the streets, the local police poured oil or molasses on them.

Tilmon began to sweat as he watched the police billy-club the helpless victims. Most of the people were black. Many of them were young children.

"Get 'im, get 'im," shouted a stringy-haired Texan.

"Man, look at that nigger run." The movie showed a ten-year-old boy trying to escape the police.

A knot began to grow in Tilmon's stomach.

Watching a high-power water hose blast a man up into the air and cartwheel him across the street, Tilmon thought he would vomit. He held his hand over his mouth and prayed for control.

"Atta boy, sic 'im, sic that nigger," the Texan yelled as a police dog lunged into the crowd and bit a screaming young girl.

Tilmon vowed that if he ever had the authority, he would forbid the use of dogs in crowd control.

When the lights went on, the instructor took out a cattle prod. Battery operated, it looked like an ordinary billy club with a flat end.

"In order for this to work, it has to penetrate meat. This is not a toy. If you want to test it, just give yourself a quick tap on the palm of your hand."

The stringy-haired Texan moved next to Tilmon. "Let's see if this works, O'Bryant. " He plunged the cattle prod into Tilmon's side.

Tilmon swung the man around by his shoulder. "You try that again and I'll break your neck."

"Sorry, O'Bryant," the Texan said. "I was just joking."

Apart from the riot-control incident, Tilmon enjoyed his classes at Quantico.

When the group returned to Washington they found that a lecture on the use of police dogs had been set up at the District of Columbia K-9 Corps barracks.

"O'Bryant, you're a Washingtonian. What's the best route?"

Tilmon sat down and drew a map. Handing it to the instructor, he said, "I'll meet you there."

When he reached the kennels, Tilmon was amazed to find that all his classmates had arrived ahead of him.

110

"Welcome to the 'Dog House,'" said Eugene Barksdale, the secretary of the class. "Fine guide you are. They were tearing up the street that you told us to take. We had to detour around and got lost. We still beat you!"

Tilmon couldn't concentrate on the lecture. Here he was, a native Washingtonian, a former cab driver, and he had given poor directions. He was mortified.

The next day in class, Jim Cotter mounted the stage. "I'm sorry to interrupt the instruction, but someone has committed a very serious offense. In the thirty-five years that this Academy has been in operation, this is the first time that this has occurred. Not only was this officer guilty of wrongdoing, but he gave false advice and caused other officers to go astray. Mr. Hoover, Mr. Dalby, and I have come to the conclusion that a hearing is in order. If the class agrees, suitable punishment will be enforced."

Each member of the class became concerned.

Jim Cotter paused and looked around the room. "Tilmon O'Bryant, will you step forward to hear the charges against you?"

A sharp pain shot through Tilmon's head. What had he done? His stomach tightened into a hard ball. Forcing his limp legs to move toward the stage, he slowly climbed each step. What would the chief say? A fine representative he was! This was the end of his career as a policeman.

Jim Cotter's face was stern. "Never before have we felt it necessary to try a fellow officer. I hope that you are aware of the seriousness of this situation. Not only did you personally do wrong but by your poor counsel caused others to follow you."

Stopping to sip some water, Jim continued. "However, because of your good record and because of the high regard in which your fellow classmates hold you, I hereby hand down the following sentence: For failure to give proper directions and thereby leading all your classmates astray, I hereby sentence you to continuously carry this instrument."

He handed Tilmon a ten-cent compass and slapped him on the back. The class laughed and applauded.

Looking very relieved, Tilmon held the compass in his raised right hand. "I hereby promise never to give any directions without first consulting my punishment."

"You've had the theory part of criminal investigation," the instructor said to them all. "Today you're going to solve a triple murder." He motioned toward the stage. Three bodies were sprawled across a "living room" floor. A pistol lay next to one of the bodies. "Gather all the evidence.

The late director of the FBI, J. Edgar Hoover, looks on as Lieutenant O'Bryant receives his diploma from the FBI National Academy

When everyone is finished, Kash, you go outside and make a plaster cast of the footprints; Ross, you draw the diagrams."

Tilmon walked around the "living room." Bending down to check the position of the bullet wounds, he drew back. These were not dummies. These were real bodies. In order to create as accurate a situation as possible, the FBI had used cadavers!

When everyone had finished, the instructor said, "I'd like to appoint one man to do a critique and two or three others to help him." He looked around the classroom.

Tilmon's head began to throb. What was a critique? Suppose the instructor called on him. Tilmon didn't know whether a critique was the name of a salad dressing or a new kind of autopsy. Too embarrassed to raise his hand and ask what the word "critique" meant, Tilmon prayed that the instructor would overlook him.

"Okay, Higgenbotham," the instructor said. "You do the critique. And put every detail into your report. Don't skip a thing."

Tilmon sighed. So a critique was a critical report. Mama was right. Education was like money in the bank. It was there right up in your head if you ever needed it. As soon as he finished the Academy course, he was going to work toward a college degree.

After graduating from the FBI Academy, Tilmon returned to duty in the Second Precinct.

Although he had had no time to study, he took the examination for captain. The FBI course, with its emphasis on police management and organization, had been excellent preparation for the test. When the results were posted, Tilmon's name was first on the list!

Congress, worried about crime in Washington, voted the money for a larger police force. With more patrolmen the

113

Chief Layton presents FBI certificate to Detective O'Bryant

department would need more officers. Tilmon had qualified himself for the opportunity that would be knocking.

Making good on his vow to obtain a college degree, Tilmon enrolled in a psychology course. When the instructor discussed the psychology of the ghetto, only Tilmon agreed with his analysis.

"O'Bryant, you seem to know more about the subject than I do. Next week, I'd like you to teach the course."

Tilmon stood before the class and gulped. "I don't have a college degree, but I do have forty-four years' experience being a black man—"

When Tilmon "told it like it is," the white students found

114

it difficult to believe that there were two standards of police enforcement, one for blacks and one for whites.

"There has to be a change, or there will be more and more street incidents," Tilmon emphasized. "Now I'm not advocating giving the Negro any advantage, but neither am I advocating giving him any extra disadvantage. You have to have a system of equal justice under the law, or there isn't any justice and soon there won't be any law."

Tilmon's lecture was so successful that he was asked to teach a course in police science at the Washington Technical Institute.

The high school dropout had become a college instructor!

18

CAPTAIN O'BRYANT

"Congratulations!" Michael and Klevin shouted. Tilmon's appointment as captain had just been announced. He was now Supervisor of Detectives in the Sixth, Tenth, and Thirteenth Precincts. These predominantly black areas were the "hottest" in the District of Columbia.

"Boy, my dad will have even more stories to tell," Klevin boasted to his classmates.

On his first day Tilmon called in all the detectives. "Even though I am a captain, I will not attempt to pull rank. Respect and cooperation are reciprocal. I am always open for advice, and I am always willing to help. But don't tell me *how* you're going to solve a case, just do it."

Carefully observing the work of all the men in the three precincts, Tilmon noticed that big, husky Mike Bello of the undercover Tactical Force was quick to dig up information and apply it. The Tactical Force men wore no uniforms. Dressed like the people in the community, they were undercover policemen, not plainclothesmen.

Sometime ago, handsome, black-haired Mike had been sent before the Police Trial Board for cursing a sergeant. He paid his fine, but the department refused to forget his offense. Despite his excellent undercover work, the department was not about to promote the hot-tempered Italian-American.

A vacancy occurred for a plainclothesman.

116

Mayor Walter E. Washington announces
Tilmon's appointment as captain

Tilmon went to his superior, Inspector Stargel. "Inspector, I'd like to promote Mike to plainclothesman. He's done some good police work, and he doesn't watch the clock."

"You can't have him. He was disrespectful to a police officer."

"He paid for that. You can't punish a man the rest of his life. I know he'll do a good job."

Stargel was adamant. "You can't have Mike. Find someone else."

"Inspector, you asked me to do a job. Don't ask me to build a house without boards and nails. Mike's good timber. I want him."

"You can't have Mike, O'Bryant."

117

"Then I won't take anyone," Tilmon insisted. "The position will stay open."

A few months later, the inspector was transferred. Tilmon appointed Mike Bello a plainclothesman.

Mike came to Tilmon. "Thanks, you're the first one who has ever taken an interest in me. Everyone else has been down on me."

"The only way to thank me is to continue to do good work. I'd like to see you study for the police exams and take the test. You have ability. Just play it cool and control your temper."

Throughout the police department, Tilmon was known for his ability to question suspects. Other divisions often asked him to interrogate people.

One day the captain of the Homicide Squad telephoned Tilmon. "O'Bryant, you're a pretty good talker. We have some suspects in a murder case that we can't break down. There's a fellow at the Receiving Home who knows something, but my men can't get him to talk. How about going out there and seeing what you can do?"

Tilmon drove over to the Receiving Home.

The young man entered the reception room. "Look, officer," he mumbled, glancing down at the cracks between the floorboards. "The police bothered me and my family three times." He pointed to his highly polished shoes. "They stepped all over my loafers and scratched them. You're just like the others. I'm keeping my mouth shut."

Tilmon pulled up two wooden chairs. "Have a seat."

Turning his chair around, Tilmon straddled it and folded his arms across the top. For three hours, Officer O'Bryant talked about baseball and all the World Series games that he had seen.

His lips pressed together and his hands clasped across his chest, the boy counted the cracks in the floor.

Lt. Tilmon O'Bryant escorts President Johnson
to church

Finally, he raised his eyes. "I know somethin', but I ain't
took no part in it."

"Look, this is a vicious murder. You owe it to society to
help solve this crime."

"Okay," the boy agreed. "I'll tell you everythin' I know,
if you promise you won't ever come near my house again
and won't tell who told you."

"I don't know whether I can promise that. This is a
murder case. Let me check with the head of the Homicide
Squad." Tilmon went to the phone.

"Okay, give him your promise." The head of the squad swore.

The boy looked at Tilmon, sizing him up. "Let me go home and change. Then I'll come down to headquarters and talk."

"Okay, I'll drive you home and wait for you."

"No, I don't want no policeman around my house," he insisted.

In an hour the young man arrived at headquarters. Furnishing all the details of the crime, he even told Tilmon where to find the murder weapon.

Tilmon turned the information over to the head of the Homicide Squad. "Is there anything else I can do?"

"No, thanks, O'Bryant. I'll let my men handle the case from here out," the captain said.

The next day the captain called Tilmon. "We can't break down the suspects. Pick up the informant and let him confront them."

"I don't see how I can do that. I promised that I would protect the informant. That man's life won't be worth anything."

"It doesn't make any difference what you promised," the captain shouted. "Bring him in."

"I have to live in this 'street,' " Tilmon insisted. "I can't do that. If word gets out that I can't be trusted, I won't be able to solve anything. And I'm not going to give a man a death sentence."

"And I'm not going to let a murder case go out the window because of a promise you made to a thief." The captain roared over the phone, "You better get the kid, or I'll send you to the Police Trial Board."

"Then send me to the Trial Board. I made a promise and I'm going to keep it." Tilmon paused. "Captain, do you mind if I come down and talk to those suspects?"

"Go ahead," the head of the Homicide Squad said.

After forty-five minutes, Tilmon walked out of the lockup room. "Send in a secretary. I have their confessions."

Even though his work as a supervisor kept him busy, Tilmon still found time to organize the 1967 police examination review course. He was pretty lucky—not only was he a captain but his success had motivated more and more black men.

In the middle of the course, Chief Layton called Tilmon down to headquarters.

"O'Bryant," the red-haired chief said, "you'll have to stop teaching the course. As a captain, you help to make up the questions for the exam. It wouldn't be fair to have you know some of the questions in advance."

"But, chief, I would never reveal them to my class."

"Sorry, O'Bryant, the department has ruled on it." Ignoring Tilmon, Chief Layton picked up the phone and began to dial.

Tilmon brought Jeff the news. "They are just afraid of too many black men getting ahead. It's a rotten break."

"Yeah, when you went to the FBI and couldn't teach the '65 class, the course just fell apart," Jeff recalled. "Your personality really held it together."

Tilmon concentrated on making his district the best in the department. He was always "on top" of his detectives. In one case, a thief walked into Dickey Cleaners. Waving a jagged-edge Coke bottle, he shouted at the cashier, "Empty the register."

When he left, the frightened woman described the man as "small, with an odd-looking nose and a sad-sack expression on his face. He didn't look like a hardened criminal. And he threw the Coke bottle on the floor after I gave him the money."

Tilmon picked up the broken bottle and took it to Private Jones at the fingerprint laboratory. Following a hunch, he checked the recent jail releases. As he fingered through the

121

file, he came across the picture of a man with a forlorn, "I just lost my best friend" expression.

The prints in the file matched those on the bottle.

Tilmon returned to the precinct and called husky James C. Butler. "Here's the information and here's his address. Pick him up."

At the end of the seven A.M. to three P.M. shift, Detective Butler called in. "Captain O'Bryant, he hasn't shown up yet. How long do you want me to look for the guy?"

"Until you find him." Tilmon believed in staying with a case until it was finished. He drove himself and his men hard.

Eleven o'clock that evening, a weary Detective Butler walked into the station house. The handcuffed man accompanying him wore a sad, sad-sack expression.

When Congress voted funds for a metropolitan police force of thirty-one hundred men, President Johnson appointed Patrick Murphy as Director of Public Safety. Mr. Murphy was a civilian, and the higher-ups in the police department were not happy with this arrangement. Feeling that there was some reason for the small number of black men on the force, Mr. Murphy thought an investigation was necessary.

He asked Chief Layton, "If you ever did anything wrong, who's the one man on the force you wouldn't want to investigate you?"

Chief Layton laughed. "Captain Tilmon O'Bryant. He's black, but he's relentless when it comes to tracking someone down."

"Then I'd like him assigned on temporary duty to my office. There's something wrong with the hiring policies. Only 10 percent of the policemen are black, and the city is 75 percent Negro."

Chief Layton looked Patrick Murphy straight in the eyes.

122

"You won't make any friends on the force and neither will O'Bryant."

Tilmon reported to the personnel office at headquarters. Grudgingly, the department found a narrow plasterboard-partitioned office. The gray metal desk was as dreary and cold as his reception. Everyone was "too busy" to talk to him.

Not afraid to work overtime, Tilmon checked each personnel file. Over eight hundred black applicants had passed both the physical and the written examinations. Why had these men never been appointed to the force? Tilmon began to ask questions.

Before too many days had passed, the Deputy Chief of the Detective Bureau called Tilmon up to the fifth floor. Leaning back in his chair, he said, "I hear that you're making an investigation for Mr. Murphy. The department isn't too happy about that."

"Chief, I'm just trying to develop a procedure to fill our allotted quotas. Mr. Murphy is also concerned about hiring more black men."

The deputy chief sat up straight in his chair. He pointed the eraser end of a pencil at Tilmon. "Whatever survey or report you make, give me a copy first and let me screen it."

Tilmon looked at him. "I don't see how I can do that. If you asked me to do a job, I couldn't give a sergeant a copy before I turned it over to you."

The official slid open the desk drawer and placed the pencil inside. Snapping the drawer shut, he said, "O'Bryant, I could take your police cruiser away from you. I could put it to better use than having it used for running errands for Mr. Murphy. You're getting too smart and you're getting too many friends. You're too much of a symbol."

"Sir, you always said that I did an outstanding job. If that's true, then I'm the kind of officer you want other black officers to look up to. You take your cruiser. I have some principles that are not for sale at any price."

Tilmon walked toward the door.

The deputy chief stared at him. "Okay, O'Bryant. Get out of here and keep that car. You and your reporter friends would make mincemeat out of me if I took it away."

In five months Tilmon had filled the police quota. Despite the fact that the department had placed him "in the doghouse" he had filled all the vacancies. There was now a greater percentage of blacks on the force, and the police department was up to its authorized strength.

19

INSPECTOR O'BRYANT

Thursday, April 4, 1968.

The telephone rang. "O'Bryant, report to Number Ten. Martin Luther King has been assassinated!"

Shocked, Tilmon tumbled into his clothes. He couldn't believe it. Dr. King, the man who preached nonviolence—murdered! He strapped on his holster. The next few days would be full of heartache and trouble.

Riding downtown, Tilmon thought he was dreaming. Every detective and policeman he knew was on the road, hurrying to his assignment. Smoke filled the warm April air, stinging his nostrils. He shook his head. It was unbelievable!

The trouble had started at Fourteenth and U, Northwest. In that busy, neon-lighted Harlem of Washington, hundreds of furious people had gathered in front of the Southern Christian Leadership Conference headquarters. With the closing of stores, the area swelled with more and more people. Angry, frustrated, they spilled over the sidewalks and into the streets. Up and down the Fourteenth Street strip they marched, breaking into stores and setting fires.

All Thursday evening and Friday morning, Tilmon and Mike Bello patrolled the riot area. At Fourteenth and Monroe they pulled over to the curb. Tilmon stepped out of the car. Wherever he looked—north, south, east, or west—he saw smoke and flames.

Tears flowed down Tilmon's cheeks. What kind of society would force a man to burn in order to be heard? Tilmon wiped his eyes with the back of his hand. He shook his head in despair. No good could come of any of this.

He got back into the cruiser.

The Mayor's voice came through the radio. He had appointed Tilmon an observer. "What's happening down there, O'Bryant?"

"It's unbelievable, Mr. Mayor. The city looks like it's been hit by bombs. Crowds are running in and out of stores. They're acting like it's a holiday. There aren't enough policemen to arrest all the looters. Fires are everywhere, but the firemen can't get enough water to put them out. You'd better set a curfew. Get everyone off the streets."

Tilmon and Mike cruised down Fourteenth Street. Five small boys ran out of a Safeway Food Store. Behind them glowed a small fire. Leaping out of the car, Tilmon and Mike threw orange juice and milk on the flames.

Across the street, a liquor store, blazing like a box of lighted matches, collapsed.

Mike and Tilmon looked at each other, helpless. They shook their heads and got back into the car. On upper Fourteenth Street, Tilmon stopped. A fifteen-year-old came out of a ladies clothing store, his arms loaded with coats.

"You don't really want to steal, do you?" Tilmon asked.

"I don't know," the boy said, grasping the clothes tighter. "I just saw them laying there."

"Put them back," Tilmon ordered.

"Okay," the boy said reluctantly. He dropped the coats on the curb and walked away.

Happy, joking people strolled by. Everyone carried something. One man struggled with two portable television sets.

"Hey, man," shouted a lady with three men's suits in her

126

Captain O'Bryant observing riot-torn Fourteenth Street

Captain O'Bryant ordering a young looter to
return stolen goods

arms, "you'd better go get yours. Ain't gonna be nothin'
left."

Tilmon shook his head. "Just look at this, Mike. They
don't know what they're doing. It's like a carnival.
Everyone wants to get something for nothing."

For Tilmon and Mike, it was a seventy-two-hour, nonstop
nightmare. As soon as they put out one fire, another flared
up. While they arrested ten looters, a hundred more got
away. There were simply not enough patrolmen to control
the rioting and the looting.

President Johnson called out the National Guard to end the riots. The troops made a ring around the area. No one was allowed in or out. Tilmon shook his head. To think that the President had to send Federal troops against his people!

Driving around, Tilmon and Mike asked over and over, "How can we prevent this from happening again?"

The whole city asked the same question. Mayor Washington, Pat Murphy, the Director of Public Safety, and members of Congress held many meetings. Something had to change.

Mayor Washington decided to start his reforms in the Thirteenth Precinct. It had been the hardest hit during the riots and the police there had a reputation for brutality. A new policy was needed.

Two weeks after the riots, he called Tilmon into his office. Patrick Murphy, the Director of Public Safety, was seated beside the Mayor.

"O'Bryant," Mayor Washington said, "I'd like you to take over as captain of the Thirteenth Precinct. I need a man who has the respect of the black community."

Surprised, Tilmon did not know what to say. "Mr. Mayor, I haven't been in uniform in sixteen years. I don't know whether I can run a precinct. I'm a detective, not an administrator." He had never thought about going back into uniform.

Pat Murphy spoke up. "It's the toughest assignment in the city. We need someone who cares about people, a man not afraid to take on a challenge."

The words ran through Tilmon's head—*A man who cares.* Did he care enough to stick out his neck? . . . Oh, how he cared! . . . Every time he saw an incident of police brutality, his stomach knotted and he thought his brain would burst out of his head. Maybe he could "turn the precinct around." Maybe he could make it into a model for

129

Capt. Tilmon O'Bryant and Lt. Marshall H.
Cook hand out awards at the Metropolitan
Police Boys Club Camp, Scotland, Md.

the whole city. He had too many responsibilities not to try.
He had responsibilities to himself, to his people, and to the
force. With administrative help, he could do a good job.

Tilmon looked at the Mayor. "I'll take it on one
condition: I want Carl Profater as my sergeant."

Carl had been desk sergeant in Number Ten. He was
smart and efficient. Tilmon had often consulted him about
uniformed patrols.

A light-skinned black man, Carl wasn't too anxious to

130

work with Tilmon. He felt that Tilmon must be an "Uncle Tom." How else could a black man have gotten ahead so fast?

Tilmon soon won Carl's respect. On his first day at Number Thirteen, Tilmon called all the men together. "I want everyone in this precinct treated the same. If you'd go to the White House and put your feet on Lady Bird Johnson's table, then you can put your feet up on a welfare lady's table. This precinct includes every race and economic level. I want a washerwoman treated with the same courtesy as a senator."

Some of the white officers didn't like Tilmon's approach. They went over his head to Chief Layton. Without telling Tilmon, the chief invited them to headquarters for a meeting.

"We don't see why we have to treat niggers same as whites," one private with fifteen years' service complained.

"Yeah," another spoke up. "Every time I lock up someone, O'Bryant wants to know why. Ain't nobody ever made us accountable for our actions before."

Chief Layton listened. "Gentlemen, the Mayor appointed O'Bryant to be in charge of the Thirteenth. Since he's not doing anything wrong, I can't remove him. You may not like having a black man over you, but what he's doing is right."

Sixty percent of the white officers transferred out of Number Thirteen. The department replaced them with inexperienced rookies.

Tilmon refused to get upset. He told Carl, "We're better off. With new men, we can train them our way. We're going to turn around the reputation of this precinct. We're going to be known for our fairness and our responsibility to the community."

A crippled girl, Ardelle Burton, lived across the street from the station house. Although confined to a wheelchair,

131

Ardelle had a smile for everyone. Her mother worked, and she was left alone before and after school.

"Mrs. Burton," Tilmon said, "carry Ardelle over here every morning. She can wait in the precinct for the school bus."

Some of the officers grumbled. "We're not baby-sitters."

"We're here to serve the community," Tilmon replied. "That child will be safer here than in the house by herself."

Even the gruffest policeman came to admire Ardelle's cheerfulness. The Thirteenth Precinct adopted her as their mascot.

Before he died, Martin Luther King had planned a Poor People's March on Washington. Thousands of poor were to march on the capital and demand "an end to hunger in America." They would ask their senators and representatives to pass laws to provide more jobs, better housing, and adequate health care.

The plea was simple: Give us a chance to build a better life.

Dr. King's death did not stop the Poor People's March. Led by a mule-drawn wagon train, the poor marched into the city. From all over America they came: feathered Indian chiefs, overalled farmers, open-shirted Mexican-Americans, ragged ghetto dwellers, and lean men from the hills of Appalachia.

Under the direction of the Southern Christian Leadership Conference, they came to build "Resurrection City." Within view of the Lincoln Memorial, three thousand people pitched tents and threw up shacks of plywood and plastic.

Despite the hopes of the marchers, Resurrection City seemed doomed. Constant rain turned the neat green park into a slippery mess of mud. Housekeeping was difficult. Trash floated all over the grounds. More often wet than dry, the marchers suffered from colds and infections.

132

The attitude of Congress was as dampening as the May rain. The poor were still "poor relations." Their needs were ignored. No new laws were passed.

The leaders could not maintain discipline. Fights broke out in the camp. Passersby, on their way to work, were mugged. Many volunteers as well as residents were robbed and beaten.

Most of the marchers became discouraged. They packed up and left.

After six weeks, the District government asked everyone to leave Resurrection City. The leaders refused. The government issued orders to tear down the shacks and the tents.

Eviction Day, three hundred tired, ragtag marchers trudged to Southern Christian Leadership Conference headquarters at Fourteenth and U. Bewildered, they stood there with their bundles and satchels. What were they to do? How were they to get back to Alabama, New Mexico, Oregon? They were frightened in this strange city.

The leaders could not give them immediate help. Transportation would not be available until the next day.

The marchers became confused. Where were they to spend the night? How were they to eat?

Local militants slipped into the crowd. Again, Fourteenth Street stirred with anger and frustration.

The patrolman raced to the call box.

Chief Layton phoned Tilmon. "O'Bryant, things are getting tight at Fourteenth and U. Go up there and prevent a riot."

"Chief, I'm only a captain," Tilmon protested.

"I don't care if you're a corporal. The Mayor says you're the only man those people will talk to. Get your tail up there."

Tilmon raced over to Fourteenth and U. He had to keep the situation from exploding. Two blocks away, the hated

Special Operations Division stood alerted. If he failed, they would throw tear gas into a terrified mob. The whole street would become a battleground.

Getting out of the squad car, Tilmon edged through the crowd. Carl Profater followed.

"Pig," a man shouted, aiming a brick at Tilmon.

"He ain't no pig. He's a brother," a cook from Mama's Carry-Out Shop yelled. "Cool it, man."

Tilmon walked over to the Reverend Walter Fauntroy. Mr. Fauntroy, a Southern Christian Leadership Conference leader, was trying to calm the mob.

"Mr. Fauntroy, get those people out of here," Tilmon ordered.

"Brother, how can I do that?" Mr. Fauntroy glanced at the large crowd. "I won't have any transportation until tomorrow."

Tilmon thought a minute. "I'll get you police buses. Take everyone up to Howard University. The Mayor will see that they're fed."

A couple of phone calls brought the buses.

Using a bullhorn, Mr. Fauntroy shouted, "All those people who were part of Resurrection City, board the buses. We're going to Howard University for chow."

Relieved, the marchers picked up their bundles and climbed aboard. The crowd broke up.

Later, Carl joked, "Looks like the Thirteenth Precinct would go out of business without Fourteenth and U."

Tilmon wiped his forehead. "Sure, just do away with ghettos, give everyone a meaningful job, and we'll have no problems. I'll buy that."

Two months after Tilmon took over, an old man in patched overalls shuffled into the station. "I'd like to talk to Cap'n O'Bryant, please."

The sergeant looked up. "What's your problem, Pop?"

"It's personal. I want to see the cap'n." His wrinkled black face had seen many hard years.

The old man climbed the steps to Tilmon's office.

Timidly, he waited at the open door.

Tilmon stepped out from behind the gray metal desk. "Come on in. What can I do for you?"

The man hesitated. Then he stuck out a gnarled, callused hand. "Son, I just want to shake your hand."

A tear slid down his nose as he held Tilmon's hand. "God bless you, Son. That's all I want to say."

The old man bowed, and with a shy smile, backed out of the door.

Trouble punched no time clock. All during the long, humid summer of 1968, Tilmon and Carl slept at the station house.

Mary complained, "It's not fair to me and to the boys. We never see you. I don't feel like I have a husband."

Tilmon frowned. "Mary, I'm a policeman twenty-four hours a day. If an emergency strikes, I want to get there fast."

She started to cry. "The police department is more important to you than our marriage."

One sticky hot evening a little past twelve, another Signal Thirteen flashed over the wire. "Urgent! Crowd gathering at Fourteenth and U. One man on ground. Policeman and dog standing over him. Situation explosive."

Tilmon tumbled out of his army cot. He sped to Fourteenth and U. A large circle of people had gathered in front of the liquor store. Tilmon shouldered his way into the center. The face of the fallen black man had turned ash white. The growling German shepherd strained at his leash, anxious to attack.

Cursing, the crowd threatened the officer.

"Put the dog back in the cruiser," Tilmon ordered. He

turned toward the Special Operations Division men waiting in the shadows. "All of you, get out of here."

When they left, Tilmon asked, "Brothers, what's the trouble?"

"We's all upset. We was protestin' the killin' of Slack Lawson by two white officers. Seems like nothin' bein' done 'bout it," a community relations worker explained.

A short, stocky lady with an African *gele* twined around her head pushed through the crowd. "Usin' dogs on us, just like we was animals. Ain't no way to treat a brother, nohow."

"I agree with you, sister. I'm going to talk to the chief and get him to stop using dogs in crowds." Tilmon looked around. "Anyone who wants to can come on over to the station house. It's never too late to talk, and maybe we can get this thing together."

The next morning Tilmon went to see Chief Layton. "The Special Operations Division had their dogs in my precinct last night. Either give me control over those men or keep them out. Any respect and goodwill I build up, they come in and tear down."

Chief Layton stared at Tilmon from across the wide mahogany desk. He had never heard of such a demand. "I can't give you control over someone else's men!"

"But it's my precinct. I'm the coach. I gotta pick the team. If you want me to do a good job, then keep the SOD out."

"Sorry, O'Bryant, I need the SOD up there as a threat." He saw the shocked look on Tilmon's face. "But I will promise to ban the use of dogs in crowd-control."

Angered, Tilmon strode out of the carpeted office. Did the department really want him to do a good job? Were they just playing with the idea of building good community relations? He wished he could really operate the precinct the way he wanted.

Once again, the frustration knotted his stomach and pounded his head. He thought his brain would shoot out of his skull.

A few days later, Patrick Murphy called Chief Layton and Tilmon into his office. The two men sat in orange armchairs opposite each other.

Murphy wasted no time. Looking at Layton, he said, "John, let me ask you one thing. Are you going to let Tilmon run his precinct or are you going to let the SOD run it?"

Layton's face turned as red as his hair. "Okay, Pat, you and the Mayor win. I'll pull out the SOD."

Gradually, the Thirteenth Precinct began to gain a reputation for fairness.

Tilmon confided to Carl, "We've got a lot of work to do, but I feel like we're doing a job. The people are beginning to respect the department. I really feel we can bring law with justice to this community."

20

HOLD YOUR HEAD UP HIGH

The threat of another riot hung over the warm, sweaty Washington summer. Like the lightning in a summer thunderstorm, trouble flashed and stabbed at the hot center of Fourteenth Street. Over and over, Tilmon and his officers rushed to put out the sparks. The summer passed without flaming incident.

Brisk October winds blew in a calmer, more relaxed feeling. The immediate danger seemed past.

Pleased with Tilmon's success, the Mayor called him into his office. "O'Bryant, you've done a good job! I'm promoting you to Inspector. You're now Supervisor of the Thirteenth and Second Precincts."

Tilmon was dumbfounded. He wondered what to say. For the first time in his life, he did not want to be promoted. He rubbed his index finger along the side of his nose. How do you say no? "Mr. Mayor, I'm honored, but I've only been in the Thirteenth for eight months. There's still a lot to be done."

The Mayor walked over to the map opposite his desk. "I need you loose, O'Bryant. You're too tied down as Captain of the Thirteenth. I want you available as a trouble-shooter." He waved his hand over the map. "You're one of the few cops that the people will talk to."

Tilmon hesitated. Every time he mastered one job, he got thrown into another.

138

"What do you say?" the Mayor asked. His glance fell on the crowded appointment book at his elbow.

"I've never refused a challenge," Tilmon admitted. "I'll do the best I can."

Tall, slender Shirley O'Neill replaced Tilmon as Captain of Number Thirteen. Like Tilmon, he believed in working with the community.

The other captain under Tilmon's supervision had different feelings. When Tilmon walked into the old red-brick station house, the captain nodded, but did not shake hands.

Taking the gray metal chair opposite the captain's desk, Tilmon said, "Captain, I want every one of your officers held accountable for the arrests he makes. If a man is locked up, I want to know why."

The captain's right hand fiddled with a box of paper clips. For a long time he stared at a spot on the ceiling. Finally he opened his mouth. "Inspector—Inspector"—he almost choked on the title—"O'Bryant, you're—you're, well, you're different. But—but most niggers, they—they have to be locked up to control them. It's for their own good, you understand."

Tilmon held in his fury. "Captain, I'll listen to everything you have to say, but I'm the supervisor. I make the final decision. I expect you to abide by it." He picked up his hat and walked out.

A few days later, Chief Layton had a visitor.

His face flushed with anger, the captain banged his fist on the desk. "John," he said to the chief, "we've been friends a long time. But it ain't right, havin' a nigger give me orders." The veins on the side of his head stood out in an ugly blue ridge.

"Simmer down," the chief ordered. "The Mayor put O'Bryant in that slot. There's nothing I can do."

The captain stared at the orange carpet. He inspected

139

the ceiling. He studied his highly polished shoes. He didn't
know what to do. It was enough to make a man quit!

Defeated, he stood up and walked toward the door.
Layton called him back. "You may not like taking orders
from a black man, but O'Bryant is fair. You'll have to learn
to work with him."

As inspector, Tilmon missed the daily excitement of the
streets. Occasionally his "Bell Boy" pocket radio would

Patrick Murphy, Civilian Director of Public
Safety, congratulates the newly appointed
inspectors: John M. Thot, Robert S. Shuttle-
worth, John Dials, and Tilmon B. O'Bryant

buzz with emergency orders. Tilmon would race to the hot spot.

On one call, he thought first before responding.

The "Bell Boy" repeated the message. "Crowd gathering at Fourteenth and U. Heading for Mayor's house. Plan to hold rally there to protest shooting of black man by white cop."

What was the best way to handle this situation? Tilmon wondered. A marching mob picks up more and more people. Along the way, windows get smashed and looting begins. Why not keep the crowd in the precinct? Let the Mayor meet with them at the station house?

Tilmon talked to the Mayor. He agreed. In a few minutes the Mayor drove up to the precinct.

Yelling and shouting, the crowd gathered around the stocky, neatly dressed Walter Washington.

Arthur Waskow, a white civil rights leader, opened the rally. "Elijah Bennett was killed for the crime of jaywalking—he was shot because he crossed the street against a traffic light. Are we gonna' stand for that kind of racist stuff? We want justice!"

Waskow thrust the microphone in front of Mayor Washington's face. "Here's your 'colonial governor.' Let's see what he has to say."

"Yeah, 'Tom,' what you got to say for yourself?" a mini-skirted student shouted.

Everyone pushed closer to the Mayor. Tilmon and Captain O'Neill watched, ready to step quickly between the Mayor and the crowd.

Before the Mayor could answer, bushy-bearded Waskow grabbed the microphone out of his hands. "I'll tell you what we want. We want community control of the police."

Mayor Washington looked at the angry, unruly mob. "You want something I can't give you, and you know it.

141

This is my city too. I want to do what's right, but we've got to work together."

Again, tall, big-bellied Waskow grabbed the microphone out of the Mayor's hands. "Now, listen . . ."

An enormous black man, taller and broader than Waskow, pushed his way through the crowd. Seizing the microphone, he growled, "Cool it, brothers. Either show the Mayor some respect or get lost. He may not be doin' the greatest job, but at least he's black." The man turned toward Waskow. "We don't need no white man leadin' the bandwagon."

Waskow took the microphone. "Thank you, brother."

"I'm not your brother," the man snapped, taking the microphone back. He turned to the people. "Now let's get this thing together. Let's rap with the Mayor and see what we can do."

For a half hour, the Mayor talked with the people. Satisfied, the crowd dispersed.

Tilmon and Captain O'Neill walked back into the station house.

"Guess it's back to robbery reports," Tilmon remarked.

"Wanna bet?" the desk sergeant said, handing them a message. "A Signal Thirteen just came in. There's another rally at Fourteenth and U. Two parked trucks are blocking the intersection. Stokely Carmichael and the big boys are leading this one."

Tilmon and Captain O'Neill rushed over to Fourteenth Street.

Black Power leaders Stokely Carmichael, Floyd McKissick, and H. Rap Brown stood in front of the New School for Afro-American Thought. As the two officers watched, people poured out of the shops and spilled into the street.

The three men grinned when they saw Tilmon and Captain O'Neill approach.

"Afternoon, brothers," Stokely said. He wore his usual green army fatigue jacket.

"Now what's the problem, brother?" Tilmon asked.

"Get your honkie police out of here," Stokely said, pointing to the two white policemen who were trying to reach the parked trucks. The crowd blocked their way. Cursing and screaming, they threatened to attack the officers.

Mayor Washington, Julian Dugas, Inspector

143

Tilmon quickly ordered the two policemen to leave the area. He turned to Stokely. "Okay, now what's the problem?"

"We're having a parade," Stokely grinned. He twirled a toothpick around in the corner of his mouth. "If this were the Rotary Club, you'd block off traffic for their parade."

Tilmon watched the October wind catch a piece of paper and blow it against the side of a building. He thought a few minutes. More and more people flowed into the street. Horns honked. A group of laughing men moved toward the corner liquor store.

Stokely chewed on his toothpick and smiled.

"All right, brother," Tilmon agreed. "We'll reroute traffic. You can have your parade."

"Right on, Stokely," a booted construction worker yelled.

Stokely grinned and waved his clenched fist in the air.

H. Rap Brown began to speak.

Tilmon and Captain O'Neill moved among the crowd, listening to complaints. The community relations workers also talked with the people.

Three hours later, the "parade" was still in progress. Soon rush-hour buses would push more and more people into Fourteenth Street. It was time to end the "parade."

Tilmon walked over to Stokely. "Mr. Carmichael, it's time to break it up."

"Parade ain't over," Stokely said, nodding toward Chuck Stone, who was speaking.

"Mr. Carmichael," Tilmon repeated, "you're black and I'm black. This ain't no way for a brother to behave against a brother. I've let you have your parade. Now get these people out of here. Another riot won't help anybody."

Stokely twirled the toothpick around in his mouth. "What will you do if I don't."

"Just get them out of here," Tilmon commanded.

Resting the toothpick in the corner of his mouth, Stokely looked at Tilmon. He glanced at all the people gathered around Chuck Stone. His eyes came back to Tilmon.

For several minutes, the two men stared at each other. The crowd pushed closer to Chuck Stone.

"Burn, baby, burn," a group of teen-agers began to chant. "Come on, Stokely, let's give it to 'Charlie.'"

Fourteenth Street confrontation with Charles Cassel and Chuck Stone

Tilmon waited, his eyes never leaving Stokely's face.

Suddenly, Stokely turned to H. Rap Brown and Floyd McKissick and said, "Okay, fellows, let's get moving."

The three leaders walked down the street. The crowd broke up.

Tilmon and Captain O'Neill rode back to the station house.

A street cop, Tilmon grew restless as supervisor. There was no challenge to reading reports. He missed the quick-witted demands of the street. There, each situation required a swift, instinctive response.

He felt boxed in, as though the department had put him on a high closet shelf and locked the door. True, he had made a few enemies. Many of the ranking officers had been displeased with his investigation of hiring policies. Others resented his fair treatment of black people.

Had he reached a dead end? In a year he would have his college degree in adult education. Was it time to look for another job?

A call from Patrick Murphy, the Director of Public Safety, made him forget his problem.

"Tilmon, I'm having you transferred. You're now Director of Personnel."

"Personnel?" Tilmon asked. "I have no training in personnel work. I wouldn't know where to begin."

Murphy waved his hand. "I need a man with a sharp nose. There's something wrong at the hiring level. We're not getting enough black men. I need an old-fashioned detective to find out why. Go into the personnel office and see what you can uncover."

"I'll be as welcome as the Lord in hell," Tilmon replied. "But I'll do the best I can." Here was another chance to fight prejudice, even if it was from behind a desk. A man had to use whatever tools he could.

The first day on his new job, Tilmon noticed a round file-card stand. It held both orange and white cards. He glanced at the woman in charge of the file. "This certainly is handy." He flipped a few cards, "Incidentally, why are some of these cards orange and some white? Can't the department afford all white cards?"

The clerk blushed. "I just inherited the practice of putting white applicants on white cards and black applicants on orange ones."

"Makes sense," Tilmon nodded. "You wouldn't be able to read black cards." Then he said very pleasantly, "Guess you'll have to retype all the orange ones onto white ones. The department wouldn't want to be accused of discrimination, would it?"

Pale, the secretary shook her head. "Oh, no, sir, we wouldn't."

"Thank you," Tilmon replied, "and before next week!"

Tilmon had always encouraged qualified men from Ivy City to apply for positions on the force.

"Not me," one chap said. "The recruiting office is open from eight A.M. to four P.M. I have to miss a day's work to take the exam."

Another explained, "I went down to the Civil Service Commission to take the test. I had a hard time finding the building, and the white officer was nasty. I'm not messin' around where I'm not wanted."

Tilmon issued a new order: All examinations for policemen were to be held at Cardoza and Spingarn High Schools. They were in the heart of the black areas. He also ordered that women give the examinations.

Next, Tilmon looked at the personnel department. His was the only black face. Whenever a vacancy occurred, he tried to fill it with a qualified black person.

Explaining his position to Carl Profater, he said, "I'm not

going to give a black man any advantage, but neither am I going to give him any disadvantage. Only if he is qualified will a black man get the job."

Rumors floated back to Tilmon. The higher-ups were unhappy with his changes.

Pat Murphy reassured him. "The Mayor and I are pleased with the job you're doing. Keep up the good work."

Inside the department, Tilmon uncovered many sly ways of holding back Negroes.

The recruiters always tried to attract the unemployed black man. Since most of these people were poor readers, they would fail the exam. The officials could then say there weren't enough qualified black men.

Tilmon thought, Why not go after the already employed person? Why not reach the man who had a job, but a poor-paying one.

Placing recruitment posters in food markets and using spot announcements on "black" radio stations, Tilmon reached the type of man he wanted. Hundreds applied for the job. Many of them passed the examination. Now, more blacks could be hired.

But only a small number of the qualified black men were sworn in. Something happened after a man passed the exam.

Tilmon had a hard time pinpointing the problem.

One day he telephoned a young man who had passed the test. "Why aren't you on the force?"

"I'm waiting for the department to tell me when to bring in my high school diploma. They said they would get in touch with me. It's been over three months," the young man replied.

Furious, Tilmon strode into the sergeant's office. "Why haven't you hired this guy? He's qualified!"

The sergeant had an immediate answer. "His application must be incomplete. I'll check it."

Tilmon watched him pull the file out of the cabinet.

"Yeah," the sergeant nodded. "We've been waiting for the guy to bring down his high school diploma. Shows how irresponsible he is. We wouldn't want his type on the force. Lot of people like that. Gotta be careful." The sergeant placed the yellow folder in the drawer.

"I want you to call that man and hire him," Tilmon ordered. "And I want to see the file on every person who passed the examination and hasn't been hired."

"Sir, it would take months to do that," the sergeant protested.

"I want all the files on my desk in three days. Just drop everything else."

Checking each rejected application, Tilmon found that most of them were "incomplete."

The anger screamed inside him. Tilmon called the chief clerk into his office. "How long have you been in this department?"

"Five years," the clerk answered.

"I want you to instruct all your people to check each application carefully. There are too many of these 'incomplete' forms. If they can't learn to do the job properly, they'll have to go. I want the job done, and I want it done right."

Within four months, one thousand new officers had been hired. For the first time, the department had filled all its vacancies and 38 percent of the force was now black.

Even though Tilmon felt satisfaction in creating a more representative police force, he was restless.

He was still a cop's cop. The desk was not his beat. Had he reached another dead end? Was he just marking time until retirement? What would he do if he left the force? For twenty years it had been his whole life.

Suddenly, Chief Layton resigned. The department

Chief Jerry V. Wilson administers the oath of office to Assistant Chief Tilmon O'Bryant (1973)

buzzed with rumors. Who would be the new chief of police? Who would be appointed to assist him?

The Mayor's face flashed on television. "I am appointing Jerry V. Wilson as Chief of Police. Tilmon O'Bryant will be promoted to deputy chief in charge of patrols."

Tilmon was stunned. He would be the first black man to be in charge of the twenty-two-hundred-man patrol division. Two thirds of the force would be under his command. The challenge of controlling violence and handling demonstrations would be his.

Tall, forward-looking Jerry Wilson was determined to make Washington a model of police and citizen cooperation. What a rare opportunity to help create a truly responsible police force!

Hundreds of officials and friends crowded into the departmental auditorium. Tall potted palms decorated the gilded room.

Onstage, the Mayor, the Chairman of the City Council, and police officials waited for the band to finish their selections. When Jerry Wilson rose to take the oath of office, he promised "to make this the best police department in the world."

And then it was Tilmon's turn to be sworn in. As he placed his hand on the Bible, he looked out at the audience. His sister Lillian sat in the front row, smiling and looking just like Mama. Beside her sat his brother Buddy and Nat Black. Brilliant, roly-poly Nunzio Bonaccorsy, with a fat cigar in his mouth, grinned up at him.

After the ceremony, an old friend came over to shake Tilmon's hand. "Congratulations, O.B., you've got it made."

"No," Tilmon shot back. "No black man ever has it made until every other black man in America 'has it made.' "

The friend slapped him on the back. "Man, you're joking."

At home that evening Tilmon thought about the remark. His left hand rested on a stack of envelopes. Some contained job offers. Others held requests for him to speak at conferences. He was gaining a national reputation. Tilmon O'Bryant thought back through the years.

From welfare to deputy chief. The road had been full of obstacles. But he had refused to be pushed back or down or out. He had fought back! With intelligence and hard work he had proven that a black man could succeed. He had set an example for ghetto kids. The next generation would find the jogging easier.

Had the rewards been worth the struggle?

It was time to add up the evidence. Tilmon took out a notebook and pencil. Slowly, he wrote:

"I am a black man. I am proud of it.

"I am an American. I am proud of it.

"I have worked hard. I have endured humiliation and heartbreak. But I would not let it defeat me. To let it defeat me would be to let it defeat every other black man. We have responsibilities to one another, just as America has responsibilities to us.

"I have every right to enjoy the fruits of this land. But I cannot enjoy these fruits until every other black man enjoys

The Assistant Chief and his family at swearing-in ceremony: Michael, Mrs. Jones, Lillian, Tilmon, sister-in-law Helen, and Klevin

them." Tilmon thought about the civil rights demonstrations of the sixties.

"Black is beautiful! But black pride means more than beauty. Black pride means the dignity to demand one's rights. Black pride means working and educating oneself to do the best possible job. Black pride means treating all people, regardless of color, fairly.

"Black pride means pride in the worth of all human beings."

Tilmon closed his notebook. He could almost hear Mama saying, *Hold your head up high, son, and don't ever let it down.*

POSTSCRIPT

Tilmon O'Bryant died of congestive heart failure on July 24, 1996. The obituary in the Washington Post of July 26, 1996, quoted former police chief Issac Fulwood Jr., "For me and a lot of young African-American officers, he represented hope for our future because he persevered against all odds," Fulwood said. "His death is a significant loss."

In the same obituary, Chief Larry D. Soulsby hailed O'Bryant as a "man who helped end the segregation of the department."

Chief O'Bryant's devotion to the force took its toll on his marriage to Mary Penn O'Bryant. Shortly after he became assistant chief, she obtained a divorce. A second marriage to Elinor Phelps O'Bryant also ended in divorce. At the time of his death in 1996, Tilmon was married to Deidre McKeller O'Bryant.

His son, Michael, became a lawyer and his son, Klevin, is an engineer.

OTHER BOOKS OF INTEREST

Frankl, Ron, *Duke Ellington,* N.Y. Chelsea House, 1988.

Gray, Genevieve S. *Life and Times of Frederick Douglass.* N.Y., Grossett and Dunlap, 1970.

Haskins, Jim. *I Have a Dream.* Conn., Millbrook Press, 1992.

McKissack, Patricia C. *A Long Hard Journey: The Story of the Pullman Car Porter.* New York, Walker, 1989.

McKissack, Patricia C. *The Civil Rights Movement in America from 1965 to the Present.* N.Y., Children's Press, 1987.

Meltzer, Milton, *Langston Hughes: A Biography.* N.Y., Crowell, 1968.

Patterson, Lillie, *Benjamin Banneker.* Abingdon, TN. Parthenon, 1978.

Reef, Catherine, *Benjamin Davis, Jr.* Frederick, MD., Henry Holt, 1992.

Tedards, Anne, *Marian Anderson, Singer.* N.Y. Chelsea House, 1988.

Williams, Juan, *Eyes on the Prize: America's Civil Rights Years 1954-1965* N.Y., Viking, 1987.

INDEX

155

156

INDEX

155

157